500 RECIPES FOR MAIN MEALS

by Marguerite Patten

HAMLYN
LONDON . NEW YORK . SYDNEY . TORONTO

Contents

Cover photograph by Paul Williams

Published by The Hamlyn Publishing Group Limited
London · New York · Sydney · Toronto
Astronaut House, Feltham, Middlesex, England

© Copyright The Hamlyn Publishing Group Limited 1963

Revised edition 1971
Fifteenth impression 1984

ISBN 0 600 33459 7

Printed and bound in Great Britain by R. J. Acford

Introduction

In this book you will find a large selection of recipes, both sweet and savoury, to serve at your main meals. They have been planned to be not only appetising to eat and attractive in appearance, but also to take only a reasonable amount of time in preparation. Many of them are rather unusual recipes, which you may not have tried before, and will, I hope, provide a complete change from your more familiar menus.

A well planned meal should provide a good balance of dishes, and leave you feeling satisfied but not overfed. That is why I have included a good selection of hors-d'oeuvre and soups.

As this book follows the normal course of a meal you will next find chapters on fish, meat, poultry and vegetables. You will notice, however, that the recipes have been arranged according to the various METHODS of cooking – roasting, grilling, frying, and so on, and there are special chapters on pressure cooking, casseroles and stews. The same type of divisions occur in the chapters on hot and cold desserts. I used this particular system because I thought it would be a help in enabling you to find the KIND of dish you want in the shortest possible time.

There are a couple of other general points I would like to mention. To those of you who may be relatively new to home-making and cooking, may I suggest that you plan your meals so that some of the cooking can be done earlier in the day. For example if you are planning to serve the kind of meat or fish which MUST be cooked at the last moment, choose a cold sweet which you can prepare beforehand. It is also sensible to make the fullest possible use of your cooker. For instance, if the main dish is to be baked in the oven, then choose a baked sweet which can be cooked at the same time, thus saving both time and fuel.

Unless otherwise stated all recipes provide good portions for 4 adults.

Some Useful Facts and Figures

Comparison of Weights and Measures

English weights and measures have been used throughout the book. 3 teaspoonfuls equal 1 tablespoon. The average English teacup is ¼ pint. The average English breakfast cup is ½ pint. When cups are mentioned in recipes they refer to a B.S.I. measuring cup which holds ½ pint or 10 fluid ounces. In case it is wished to translate quantities into American or metric counterparts the following give a comparison.

Liquid measure

The American pint is 16 fluid ounces, as opposed to the British Imperial pint and Canadian pint which are 20 fluid ounces. The American ½-pint measuring cup is therefore equivalent to ⅖ British pint. In Australia the British Imperial pint, 20 fluid ounces, is used.

Solid measure

British	American
1 lb. butter or other fat	2 cups
1 lb. flour	4 cups
1 lb. granulated or castor sugar	2 cups
1 lb. icing or confectioners' sugar	3½ cups
1 lb. brown (moist) sugar	2 cups
12 oz. golden syrup or treacle	1 cup
14 oz. rice	2 cups
1 lb. dried fruit	3 cups
1 lb. chopped meat (firmly packed)	2 cups
1 lb. lentils or split peas	2 cups
1 lb. coffee (unground)	2¼ cups
1 lb. soft breadcrumbs	8 cups
½ oz. flour	2 tablespoons
1 oz. flour	¼ cup
1 oz. sugar	2 tablespoons
½ oz. butter	1 tablespoon
1 oz. golden syrup or treacle	1 tablespoon
1 oz. jam or jelly	1 tablespoon

All U.S. standard measuring cups or tablespoons

To help you understand metrication

You will see from the chart that 1 oz. is approximately 28 grammes but can be rounded off to the more convenient measuring unit of 25. Also the figures in the right hand column are not always increased by 25. This is to reduce the difference between the convenient number and the nearest equivalent. If in a recipe the ingredients to be converted are 1 oz. of margarine and 6 oz. of flour, these are the conversions: 25 grammes margarine and 175 grammes flour.

The conversion chart

Ounces	Approx. g and ml to nearest whole number	Approx. to nearest units of 25
1	28	25
2	57	50
3	85	75
4	113	125
5	142	150
6	170	175
7	198	200
8	226	225
12	340	350
16	456	450

Note: When converting quantities over 16 oz. first add the appropriate figures in the centre column, not those given in the right hand column, THEN adjust to the nearest unit of 25 grammes. For example, to convert 1¾ lb. add 456 grammes to 340 grammes which equals 796 grammes. When rounded off to the convenient figure it becomes 800 grammes.

Approximate liquid conversion

¼ pint–150 ml	1,000 millilitres–1 1 (litre)
½ pint–275 ml	1 litre–1¾ pints
¾ pint–425 ml	½ litre–¾ pint plus 4 tablespoons
1 pint–575 ml	1 dl (decilitre)–6 tablespoons

Note: If solid ingredients give scant weight using the 25 unit conversion, the amount of liquid allowed must also be scant. For example, although 575 ml is nearer to 1 pint (20 fluid oz.) when making a white pouring sauce use 550 ml of milk to 25 grammes each of butter and flour for a better consistency.

Oven Temperatures

The following chart gives conversions from degrees Fahrenheit to degrees Celsius (formerly known as Centigrade). This chart is accurate to within 3° Celsius, and can therefore be used for recipes which give oven temperatures in metric.

Note: This table is an approximate guide only. Different makes of cooker vary and if you are in any doubt about the setting it is as well to refer to the manufacturer's temperature chart.

Description	Electric Setting	Gas Mark
VERY COOL	225°F–110°C	¼
	250°F–130°C	½
COOL	275°F–140°C	1
	300°F–150°C	2
MODERATE	325°F–170°C	3
	350°F–180°C	4
MODERATELY HOT	375°F–190°C	5
	400°F–200°C	6
HOT	425°F–220°C	7
	450°F–230°C	8
VERY HOT	475°F–240°C	9

Hors-d'oeuvre

Serving hors-d'oeuvre

If you are planning to serve a selection of hors-d'oeuvre, it is best to use one of the special hors-d'oeuvre trays which has a number of divisions, so that there is a separate section for each type of food. If this is not possible, you can make up individual plates on which the various types of food are attractively arranged. Since most hors-d'oeuvre are coated, during preparation, with either oil and vinegar or mayonnaise, it will not be necessary to serve these separately.

Spiced grapefruit

cooking time: 3–5 minutes

1 Halve the grapefruit in the usual way and separate the segments of fruit.
2 Spread a little butter on top, and sprinkle with spice and sugar.
3 Either heat for a few minutes under the grill or in a hot oven.

Sherry and ginger grapefruit

Put a thin slice of preserved ginger between each segment of grapefruit, sprinkle with sherry, blended with 1–2 teaspoons preserved ginger syrup; serve heated, as above, or chilled.

Melon cocktail

no cooking

you will need:
melon
fresh orange
   segments

sugar (optional)

1 Dice the melon or make balls of the pulp with a vegetable scoop.
2 Arrange in glasses with segments of fresh orange.
3 Sprinkle with sugar if wished.

Summer melon

Mix melon balls or diced fruit with halved fresh cherries, strawberries, and other summer fruits. Sprinkle with lemon juice rather than orange juice, to give a refreshing flavour, and add a very little sugar.

Florida basket

no cooking

you will need:
2 large grapefruit
2 rings pineapple
sugar

4 cherries
sprig mint

1 Prepare the grapefruit by halving and removing the segments of fruit.
2 Mix with chopped pineapple and sugar, and pile back into the halves of grapefruit.
3 Top with cherries and mint.

Melon and raspberry cocktail

no cooking

you will need:
melon
fresh raspberries

little kirsch

1 Dice the melon or make balls of the pulp with a vegetable scoop.
2 Mix with raspberries and a little kirsch.
3 Pile into glasses.

Pineapple and lemon juice

no cooking

you will need:
canned pineapple
  juice
fresh lemon juice

sprigs mint or lemon
slices

1 Mix canned pineapple juice with a little fresh lemon juice.
2 Serve in cocktail glasses, topped with sprigs of mint or slices of lemon.

Tomato orange cocktail

no cooking

you will need:

canned tomato juice
canned or fresh
    orange juice
sprigs mint
orange slices

1 Mix the juices together, using two parts tomato juice and one part orange juice.
2 Chill thoroughly with a few bruised sprigs of mint.
3 Serve in small glasses topped with orange slices.

Grapefruit and prawns

no cooking

you will need:

grapefruit
few prawns (or
    shrimps)
mayonnaise
lettuce
lemon to garnish

1 Halve grapefruit, and remove the segments of fruit.
2 Mix with a few prawns (or shrimps) and a little mayonnaise.
3 Arrange shredded lettuce in the grapefruit halves.
4 Put the fruit and fish on top, garnishing with lemon.

Avocado and prawns

no cooking

you will need:

avocado pears
prawns (or shrimps)
oil
vinegar
seasoning

1 Halve avocado pears and remove the stones.
2 Fill the centre with shrimps or prawns, tossed in oil and vinegar.
3 Serve with small forks and spoons, topping with more well seasoned oil and vinegar if wished.

Grapefruit and avocado salad

Halve and skin ripe avocado pears, then cut into slices; arrange on a bed of lettuce with segments of fresh or canned grapefruit. Top with a few prawns in mayonnaise or oil and vinegar dressing.

Prawns mornay

cooking time: 15 minutes

you will need:

½ pint cheese sauce
    (see page 88)
8 oz. prawns
lemon
parsley

1 Make the cheese sauce.
2 Add the prawns, and heat for a few minutes.
3 Divide into 4 small dishes, top with chopped parsley.
4 Garnish with wedges of lemon.

Prawns Milanaise

Make the tomato sauce, page 87, heat the prawns in this. Put in small dishes and top with grated cheese.

Smoked eel and horseradish

no cooking

you will need:

smoked eel
lettuce
lemon
horseradish sauce
brown bread and
    butter

1 Buy the smoked eel, allowing 2–3 oz. per person.
2 Remove the skin and arrange on crisp lettuce.
3 Garnish with lemon and serve with horseradish sauce and brown bread and butter.

Smoked salmon and spinach

cooking time: 15 minutes

you will need:

4 tiny tartlets cases
    (short crust pastry,
    see page 75)
approximately 8 oz.
    cooked spinach
    (frozen ideal)
little butter
1 tablespoon cream
4–6 oz. smoked salmon
lemon

1 Bake the tartlet cases in a hot oven (450°F. – Gas Mark 7) until crisp and brown.
2 Reheat the spinach with the butter and cream.
3 Arrange in the hot tartlet cases.
4 Put the smoked salmon on to cold plates, garnish with lemon.
5 At the last minute arrange the tartlet cases on the plates.

Sardines gratinées

cooking time: 5 minutes

you will need:

fingers fried bread or toast	curry powder
sardines	chopped parsley
	Worcestershire sauce

1 Fry or toast bread.
2 Arrange sardines in oil on fingers of bread.
3 Brush with oil from can, or with melted butter.
4 Sprinkle with curry powder and chopped parsley together with a few drops Worcestershire sauce.
5 Heat under the grill, and serve with crisp salad.

Salmon pyramids

no cooking

you will need:

8 oz. cooked or canned salmon	little mayonnaise
2 hard-boiled eggs	salad to garnish

1 Blend the flaked salmon with the chopped hard-boiled egg white.
2 Bind with mayonnaise.
3 Form into pyramid shapes and serve on crisp lettuce with sliced tomatoes, cucumber etc.
4 Sprinkle the finely chopped yolk over the top.

Crab mornay

cooking time: 15 minutes

you will need:

¼ pint cheese sauce (see page 88)	lemon
2 medium sized crabs	parsley

1 Make the cheese sauce, and put half of this at the bottom of 4 small dishes.
2 Cover with flaked crab meat and rest of the sauce.
3 Heat under the grill and serve with lemon and chopped parsley to garnish.

Variations:

Lobster mornay – recipe as for Crab mornay above, using flaked lobster meat.
Canned lobster could be used instead.

Seafood scallops – recipe as Crab mornay above, but use a selection of cooked or canned fish and shellfish; put into the dishes and top with tiny croûtons of fried bread.

Cod's roe pâté

cooking time: 20 minutes

you will need:

cod's roe	pepper
butter or margarine	chopped chives
lettuce	(optional)

1 If cod's roe is uncooked, steam in butter paper for about 20 minutes and allow to cool.
2 Remove from the skin and blend with a little butter or margarine and pepper.
3 Serve on crisp lettuce with brown bread and butter, or crisp toast and butter.
4 Chopped chives can be added if wished.

Variation:

Salmon pâté – use cooked salmon instead of cod's roe, but give the pâté additional flavour with lemon juice and garlic salt.

Anchovy olives

no cooking

you will need:

anchovies	brown bread and
green olives	butter

1 Wrap fillets of anchovies round olives.
2 Serve on thin fingers of brown bread and butter.

Ham rolls

no cooking

you will need:

2 oz. cream cheese	8 small strips cooked ham
2 teaspoons chopped gherkins	lettuce
2 teaspoons chopped capers	tomatoes
2 teaspoons chopped parsley	mayonnaise (optional)

1 Mix cheese with gherkins, capers and parsley.
2 Spread over the ham and roll up.
3 Serve on bed of salad, covering with little mayonnaise if wished.

Spiced tongue

no cooking

you will need:

1 small onion or few cocktail onions	1 teaspoon Worcestershire sauce
4–6 oz. cooked tongue	1 tablespoon chutney watercress

1 Chop the onion very finely.
2 Cut the tongue into neat pieces.
3 Mix with onion, sauce, and chutney.
4 Serve on bed of watercress.

Variation:

Spiced sausage – recipe as spiced tongue, above, but use cooked sausage or frankfurters.

Chicken walnut salad

no cooking

you will need:

cooked chicken	strips of red or green peppers
mayonnaise	
chopped walnuts	

1 Moisten small strips of cooked chicken with mayonnaise.
2 Add coarsely chopped walnuts.
3 Garnish with strips of pepper.

Variation:

Curried chicken hors d'oeuvre – blend a little curry powder with the mayonnaise, toss cooked rice in this, then add the chicken etc. as recipe above for chicken walnut salad.

Croque monsieur

cooking time: few minutes

you will need:

bread and butter	beaten egg
5 slices of cheese and ham	little milk
	fat

1 Make sandwich of bread and butter, with slices of cheese and ham.
2 Dip in beaten egg, mixed with a little milk.
3 Fry steadily in hot fat until crisp and golden brown on either side.
4 Serve at once.

Carrot salad

no cooking

you will need:

carrots	chives
mayonnaise	shredded cabbage
parsley	

1 Grate good sized raw carrots coarsely.
2 Blend with mayonnaise, chopped parsley and chopped chives.
3 Serve on bed of shredded cabbage.

Beetroot salad

no cooking

you will need:

cooked beetroot	chives or spring onions
oil	watercress
vinegar	

1 Dice beetroot.
2 Blend, without making too moist, with little oil and vinegar.
3 Add finely chopped chives or spring onions.
4 Serve on bed of watercress.

Variation:

Beetroot and apple salad – use equal quantities of cooked beetroot and dessert apple. Dice the beetroot and apple (peel this if wished) then proceed as recipe above.

Asparagus salad

cooking time: 20–25 minutes (if using fresh asparagus)

you will need:

asparagus tips (cooked or canned)	lettuce
oil	chopped hard-boiled egg
vinegar	

1 Toss the cooked or canned asparagus tips in well-seasoned oil and vinegar.
2 Arrange on a bed of crisp lettuce and garnish with chopped hard-boiled egg.

Mixed vegetable or Russian salad

cooking time: 10–25 minutes

you will need:

vegetables (carrots, turnips, potato, also peas, beans etc. if possible)

mayonnaise
chopped parsley

1 Dice vegetables finely.
2 Cook steadily in boiling water.
3 Drain and blend with mayonnaise while still hot.
4 Garnish with chopped parsley when cold.

Celery salad

no cooking

you will need:

crisp celery
chopped walnuts

chopped parsley
mayonnaise

1 Chop celery finely.
2 Mix with walnuts, parsley and mayonnaise.

Variation:

Danish celery salad – crumble a little Danish Blue cheese, add to mayonnaise as recipe.

Cucumber salad

no cooking

you will need:

cucumber
vinegar and seasoning or oil and vinegar

or lemon juice
chopped parsley

1 Slice cucumber thinly.
2 Blend with vinegar and seasoning or oil and vinegar or lemon juice.
3 Lift from the dressing just before serving, and top with chopped parsley.

Potato salads

cooking time: 10–25 minutes

you will need:

old or new potatoes
mayonnaise or oil and vinegar

chopped chives or grated onion
parsley
paprika pepper

1 Cook potatoes steadily until just soft – dice if wished for speedy cooking, but be careful they do not break.
2 Drain carefully, and blend – WHILE STILL HOT – with mayonnaise or oil and vinegar.
3 Blend with chopped chives or finely chopped or grated onion and chopped parsley.
4 Garnish with more parsley and paprika pepper.

Variations:

Mix dressed potatoes with:
(a) Chopped gherkins, capers and celery.
(b) Chopped celery, grated dessert apple and sultanas.
(c) Chopped celery and diced cucumber.

Tomato salad

no cooking

you will need:

tomatoes
oil
vinegar

seasoning
chopped chives or spring onions

1 Slice tomatoes thinly, and blend with oil and vinegar, season well.
2 Garnish with chopped chives or spring onions.

Variation:

Tomato and pepper salad – use 1 green and 1 red pepper to each 3 tomatoes. Prepare the tomatoes as above, then cut the peppers into thin rings, discarding core and seeds. Arrange on long dishes and garnish as above.

Cole slaw

no cooking

you will need:

crisp cabbage
sultanas
chopped nuts

mayonnaise
lemon juice

1 Shred cabbage finely.
2 Mix with sultanas, chopped nuts, mayonnaise and a little lemon juice.

Spiced cole slaw

no cooking

you will need:

crisp cabbage
lemon juice
oil
1 teaspoon chilli sauce or Worcestershire sauce

shredded red pepper
chopped gherkins
capers
chopped celery (optional)

1 Shred cabbage finely.
2 Blend with lemon juice, little oil, chilli sauce or Worcestershire sauce.
3 Mix with finely shredded red pepper, chopped gherkins, capers and chopped celery when in season.

Soups

Among the recipes which follow, you will find several of the easier-to-make soups, as well as a number of more substantial recipes, which can turn a light snack into a good main meal. When making and serving soup, remember:

1 Take a little time and trouble to garnish soups to make them look more colourful.
2 Light coloured soups, such as cream soups look attractive if both chopped parsley or paprika pepper are sprinkled over the top, or you can use very finely chopped egg yolk.
3 Dark coloured soups, such as meat soups need a light garnish. Grated cheese, chopped egg white, fried croûtons of bread are effective.
4 Always make sure the soup is very hot before serving. If you wish to keep it hot for an extended period of time, without it becoming too thick or burning on the bottom of the pan, transfer it to the top of a double saucepan.
5 A pressure cooker is an ideal way of making stock or soups, particularly those which normally need prolonged cooking. I have therefore, included recipes for pressure cooked soups.

Lentil soup

cooking time: 2 hours

you will need:

8 oz. lentils	1 teaspoon salt
seasoning	small bacon bone
3 oz. onions	strips of streaky bacon
3 pints cold water	croûtons
1–2 cloves (optional)	

1 Soak lentils overnight in water. Season.
2 Put lentils into pan with sliced onion, water, cloves, salt and bacon bone. Cook steadily.
3 When lentils are soft, sieve.
4 Rinse pan, return the purée which you can thin with stock or thicken as necessary. Season.
5 Garnish with croûtons of fried bread and crispy streaky bacon when serving.

Variations:

Curried lentil soup – blend the lentils at stage 2 in the recipe above, with 2–3 teaspoons curry powder or curry paste. Return to the pan, adding 2 oz. sultanas, pinch sugar, piece of apple and ingredients as lentil soup, continue as recipe.

Green pea soup – as recipe for lentil soup using split peas instead of lentils and omitting cloves. Cooking time 1½–2 hours.

Vegetable chowder

cooking time: 1¼ hours

you will need:

2 large potatoes	seasoning
2 large onions	good pinch celery
small piece swede	salt
small piece celeriac	bay leaf
½ clove garlic	2 pints water or white
finely diced celery	stock
pinch mixed herbs	

to garnish:

chopped watercress	little grated cheese
	paprika pepper

1 Dice all vegetables very finely, and crush garlic.
2 Put into casserole with seasoning, bay leaf and liquid.
3 Cover with lid and allow about 1¼ hours in slow oven (300°F. – Gas Mark 2).
4 Garnish with watercress, cheese and pepper.

Variations:

Vegetable cream chowder – as above but use only 1¾ pints water or stock, and add ¼ pint thin cream before serving.

Vegetable ham chowder – as for vegetable chowder above, but add 2–3 oz. finely chopped ham or boiled bacon.

Fish and vegetable chowder – continue as recipe above and cook for about 45 minutes at stage 3, then add 8–10 oz. skinned, diced, raw white fish and continue cooking. Garnish as above, but serve with wedges of lemon.

Speedy chowders – use any of the recipes above, but grate, rather than dice the vegetables, and cook in a saucepan for about 20 minutes only. In the fish and vegetable chowder, add the fish 10 minutes before serving.

Beef and onion soup

cooking time: 1½ hours

you will need:

4 medium sized onions	seasoning
1¾ pints good beef	2 slices bread
stock (or water with	2 oz. butter
beef bouillon cubes)	

1 Chop onions finely.
2 Put into casserole with stock and seasoning.
3 Cover with lid and cook for 1½ hours in slow oven (300°F. – Gas Mark 2).
4 Dice bread, fry in butter. Serve on soup.

Variation:

Paprika soup – use the recipe for beef and onion soup before, but blend 2–3 skinned, chopped tomatoes and 2 teaspoons paprika with the onions etc. at stage 2.

Chicken broth

cooking time: 2 hours

you will need:

1 large onion	2 pints water with 2
2 carrots	chicken bouillon
2 large tomatoes	cubes, or 2 pints
small pieces uncooked	chicken stock
chicken	2 oz. rice
	little chopped parsley
	seasoning

1 Dice vegetables and chicken very finely.
2 Put into casserole with other ingredients.
3 Cover with a lid and cook for 2 hours in a very slow oven (275°F. – Gas Mark 1).

Variation:

Creamed chicken broth – follow directions above, cooking either in the oven for 2 hours or for 1 hour in a covered saucepan. Sieve the soup or emulsify in a warmed liquidiser goblet, put into a pan and reheat; then add about ¼ pint thin cream and a little extra seasoning.

Minestrone soup

cooking time: 2 hours

you will need:

3 oz. haricot beans	1 dessertspoon
2 oz. quick cooking	chopped parsley
macaroni	8 oz. tomatoes (fresh
1 oz. dripping or oil	or canned)
1 finely chopped or	8 oz. chopped cabbage
grated onion	water
piece chopped celery	seasoning
	1 oz. grated cheese

1 Soak the beans for 24 hours.
2 Simmer in about 1½ pints water until soft.
3 Boil macaroni for 7 minutes in salted boiling water.
4 Heat dripping and fry the onion, celery and parsley for 5 minutes.
5 Add chopped tomatoes, cabbage and 1 pint water and bring to the boil.
6 Put in the beans, macaroni and seasoning.
7 Simmer for 30 minutes.
8 Serve sprinkled with grated cheese.

Note: This soup is very thick.

Summer soup

cooking time: 20 minutes

you will need:

1 pint bottled or	about 12 oz. mixed
canned tomato juice	vegetables
	seasoning

1 Simmer the vegetables in the tomato juice until just tender, adding a little extra water if the mixture becomes too thick.
2 Season well and serve with cheese flavoured biscuits.

Variations:

Tomato and cucumber soup – add 1 medium sized peeled cucumber to the tomato juice. Cut this into thin shreds and simmer until just tender.

Turkish cucumber soup – simmer very thin slices of peeled cucumber in the tomato juice until tender. Allow to cool, then serve topped with natural yoghourt.

Onion soup

cooking time: 15 minutes

you will need:

2 medium potatoes	½ oz. butter
bunch spring onions	seasoning
(not too large) or 2	1½ pints stock or water
good-sized onions	little cream

1 Chop both potatoes and onions very finely and toss in the butter for about 5 minutes.
2 Add seasoning, stock or water and simmer for about 5 minutes.
3 Stir well so that you break up the potatoes to thicken soup, but there is no need to sieve it.
4 Add a little cream and serve at once.

To serve: Excellent topped with grated cheese.

Cream of tomato soup

cooking time: 30–40 minutes

you will need:

1 lb. tomatoes	¼ pint water
1 onion	seasoning
2 bay leaves	1 pint thin white sauce
4 peppercorns	(see page 88)

1 Simmer the tomatoes and chopped onion together with bay leaves and peppercorns in the water until quite soft. Season.
2 Rub through a fine sieve.
3 Heat the sauce and reheat the tomato purée.
4 Take both pans off the heat and make sure the contents are not boiling.
5 Whisk together. This method stops the soup curdling.

Cream of asparagus soup

cooking time: 25–30 minutes

you will need:

1 lb. asparagus	1 onion
1 oz. butter or	seasoning
margarine	¾ pint thin white sauce
1 pint water	(see page 88)

1 Cut the asparagus into small pieces.
2 Toss in the melted butter or margarine and cook for 5 minutes.
3 Add the water and chopped onion.
4 Simmer steadily until the asparagus is very soft. Season.
5 Rub through a fine sieve.
6 Reheat the asparagus purée and add to the hot sauce.
7 Continue as with cream of tomato soup.

Creamy potato soup

cooking time: 25 minutes

you will need:

approximately	2 oz. butter
1 lb. potatoes	little cream if wished
½ pint water	chopped chives **or**
seasoning	spring onion stems
1 pint milk	

1 Grate the peeled potatoes (this saves sieving).
2 Put into saucepan with the water and seasoning and cook for about 20 minutes until very soft (watch they don't become too thick and burn).
3 Add the milk, butter, cream and lots of seasoning.
4 Bring to the boil and stir until smooth consistency.
5 Garnish with the chives or onion stems.
6 Serve with fried bread cut into small pieces.

Variation:

Onion and potato soup – grate 2 large onions and add to the potatoes at stage 1 in the soup above.

Cream of mushroom soup

cooking time: 12 minutes

you will need:

8 oz. mushrooms*	1 pint water or stock
2 oz. butter or	¾ pint milk
margarine	seasoning
2 oz. flour	

* The stems of mushrooms could be used if wished.

1 Chop mushrooms, finely, unless straining the soup.
2 Melt butter or margarine in saucepan.
3 Fry mushrooms for 5 minutes, stirring to prevent them discolouring.
4 Stir in the flour and cook for 3 minutes.
5 Remove from the heat and gradually add water and milk.
6 Bring to the boil and cook until soup thickens.
7 Season and serve.

Cheese soup

cooking time: 10 minutes

you will need:

1 small thinly sliced	½ pint stock or water
onion	½ level teaspoon salt
1 oz. butter	pinch pepper
1 oz. plain flour	4 oz. Cheddar cheese
½ pint milk	(diced small)

1 Cook the onion in the butter for a few minutes.
2 Add the flour and cook for another minute.
3 Stir in the milk and stock or water, and bring to the boil.
4 Season and simmer gently for about 5 minutes.
5 Toss in the cheese and stir without boiling until melted.
6 Serve piping hot. Cheese soup can be reheated and used the next day.

Variation:

Carrot and cheese soup – use the recipe above, but add 2 large grated carrots at stage 4. Cook for only 5 minutes so the carrots remain fairly firm in texture then continue as the recipe. If reheating the cheese soup do not allow to boil as this would make it curdle.

Artichoke soup

pressure cooking time: 20 minutes

you will need:

1½ lb. artichokes	½ oz. flour
½ pint water or white	¼ pint milk
stock	½ oz. margarine or
¼ teaspoon vinegar	butter
seasoning	

1 Wash and peel the artichokes, if large cut into halves.
2 Put into the pressure cooker with the water, vinegar (to preserve the colour) and seasoning.
3 Put on the lid and bring steadily up to pressure.
4 Lower the heat and cook for 15 minutes.
5 Allow pressure to drop then remove lid.
6 Mix the flour with the milk, sieve or mash the artichokes. *continued*

7 Return to the pan, together with the milk mixture, and bring slowly to the boil.

8 Add the margarine and any additional seasoning if necessary.

9 Cook for 2–3 minutes.

Celery soup

pressure cooking time: 20 minutes

you will need:

1 good head celery	seasoning
¾ pint white stock or water	1 oz. flour
	¼ pint milk
1 small onion	1 oz. margarine
bunch fresh herbs (tied in muslin) or pinch dried herbs	

1 Cut the celery into small pieces and put into cooker with the stock, onion, mixed herbs and seasoning.

2 Put on the lid and bring steadily up to pressure.

3 Lower heat and cook 15 minutes.

4 Continue as with recipe for artichoke soup thickening in the same way.

Haricot bean soup

pressure cooking time: 35 minutes

you will need:

8 oz. haricot beans	1 oz. flour
1 pint water	½ pint milk
2 onions	knob of butter
seasoning	

1 Soak the beans overnight.

2 Put into cooker with 1 pint of water in which they were soaked, chopped onions and seasoning.

3 Put on the lid and bring steadily to pressure.

4 Lower heat and cook for 30 minutes. If beans are very large, cook for 35 minutes.

5 Allow pressure to drop and remove lid.

6 Rub beans through a sieve and return to cooker.

7 Blend the flour with the milk.

8 Add to soup and bring to the boil.

9 Boil steadily for 3–4 minutes.

10 Add a knob of butter before serving.

Lentil soup

pressure cooking time: 17 minutes

you will need:

8 oz. lentils	1½ pints water
2–3 sticks celery	seasoning
2 medium sized potatoes	bunch herbs, or good pinch dried herbs
2 onions	¼ pint milk

1 Put all the ingredients except milk into pressure cooker.

2 Add salt, bring steadily to pressure.

3 Lower heat and cook for 15 minutes.

4 Allow pressure to drop.

5 Rub through a sieve.

6 Return to the cooker with the milk and reheat.

Fish Dishes

Choosing and cooking fish

Whatever method of cooking is used for fish, there are certain basic rules which are most important to remember:

1 DO NOT OVERCOOK fish. The moment the flesh breaks away from the skin or bones, the fish should be served.

2 DO NOT keep fish dishes waiting, since this will again overcook the fish, with a consequent loss of flavour and moisture.

3 TAKE GREAT CARE when choosing fish. When fresh, it should be firm, with no strong smell. The eyes should be bright, and scales firm and clear.

4 Shellfish should feel heavy for the weight. If they are surprisingly light, then it is certain they contain a high percentage of water, and you are not receiving good value for your money.

5 DO NOT STORE FISH FOR TOO LONG A PERIOD, EVEN IN A REFRIGERATOR.

Shallow frying fish

1 Coat the fish, if desired. For this type of frying, it is better to use seasoned crumbs and an egg, rather than a batter.

2 Make sure the fat is really hot before putting in fish.

3 Fry quickly on either side to brown the fish.

4 Then in the case of cutlets or thick pieces of fish, lower the heat to make sure it is done right through to the centre.

5 Drain well on absorbent or tissue paper before serving.

Sole meunière

cooking time: 10–15 minutes

you will need:

8 fillets sole	very little flour
seasoning	4 oz. butter
squeeze lemon juice	

to garnish:

lemon rings	chopped parsley

1 Season the fish and give a squeeze lemon juice.
2 Dust lightly with the flour.
3 Heat the butter in a pan and fry fish carefully until golden brown, BUT DO NOT OVER-COOK.
4 Lift on to hot dish.
5 Heat remaining butter in pan until really golden brown, adding little extra lemon juice if wished.
6 Pour over the fish and top with lemon and parsley.

Lemon plaice

cooking time: 8–10 minutes

you will need:

8 small fillets plaice	1 oz. flour
seasoning	1 lemon

to fry:
2–3 oz. fat

1 Wash and dry the plaice, then coat in the seasoned flour blended with the grated rind of the lemon.
2 Fry steadily in the hot fat until crisp and golden brown, then drain on absorbent paper.
3 Remove the rest of the peel from the lemon and sprinkle tiny pieces of the pulp over the fish just before serving.

Deep frying fish

1 You can use either seasoned flour, egg and bread crumbs or batter for coating.
2 Make sure the fat is really hot before the fish goes in.
3 Brown the fish quickly in the hot fat.
4 Lower the heat to make sure it is done through to the centre.

Grilling fish

1 Make certain the grill is really hot before putting the fish underneath.

2 Brush both the grid of the grill pan with fat and brush the top of the fish with fat also.
3 Cook quickly until golden brown, turning thicker pieces of fish. Always keep fish very well 'basted' with butter or fat during the grilling period.

Grilled herring and mustard sauce

cooking time: 10–15 minutes

you will need:

4 large or 8 small herrings	lemon parsley
little butter	

1 Butter the herrings well.
2 To make sure the grill pan does not smell too much of the fish, it is a good idea to put greased foil over the grill pan and put the herrings in this.
3 Grill on both sides of the fish.
4 Serve with mustard sauce, garnished with lemon and parsley.

for the sauce:

2 oz. butter	1 tablespoon mustard
1 oz. flour	1 teaspoon vinegar
½ pint water	salt

1 Heat 1 oz. of the butter in a pan.
2 Stir in the flour and cook for several minutes.
3 Blend the mustard with the water until very smooth.
4 Add to the butter and flour and bring to the boil SLOWLY, stirring until smooth.
5 Add the vinegar, extra butter and pinch salt.

Grilled fish au gratin

Grill any chosen fish and when nearly cooked press a thick layer of grated cheese over the top of the fish, together with a few soft or crisp breadcrumbs. Return to the grill and cook until the cheese melts and browns.

Steaming fish

Most fish can be steamed, if wished, but one generally chooses flat fish, such as plaice, sole, fillets of haddock etc. One of the most popular methods of steaming fish is as follows:
1 Put the fish on a large plate, add seasoning, a squeeze of lemon juice, knob of butter, then cover with a second plate. *continued*

15

2 Stand over a pan of boiling water, and cook steadily for approximately 10–12 minutes for thin fillets of fish, up to 20 minutes for whole fish or thick fillets.

3 If wished, milk can be poured over the fish before cooking, and this could be used as a basis for a sauce.

4 This method of cooking is recommended for invalids, since the fish is so easily digested. It does however look rather colourless, so that a garnish of chopped parsley, lemon etc. (if allowed), makes it more appetising.

Savoury steamed fish

Put the fish on a large plate as stage 1 above, but instead of adding seasoning and butter, cover with several tablespoons hot soup, e.g. cheese, mushroom or tomato, or any of the shellfish soups. Continue as recipe above.

Boiling or poaching fish

While the term 'boiling' is used to describe the method of cooking fish in water, the word BOIL is actually incorrect, since the fish should be cooked in water BELOW BOILING POINT. If you boil the fish it breaks and becomes dry in texture. It is therefore better to poach it gently in well-seasoned water, or fish stock. The stock is made by first cooking the bones and skin of the fish with seasoning and a bay leaf. All white fish as well as salmon and mackerel can be cooked by this method. White fish should be poached as follows:

1 Put the fish into the cold, seasoned water or stock.

2 Allow to come to about 180°F. (the point when one or two bubbles can be seen on the surface of the water).

3 Simmer steadily, allowing about 7 minutes per lb. (10 minutes if about 1 lb. only).

4 Drain carefully, and serve with melted butter or sauce.

To poach salmon

In order to keep the particular moist texture and colour of fresh salmon, it is best to wrap it in buttered or oiled paper before the poaching process. Poach salmon as follows:

1 Oil or butter a good sized sheet of greaseproof paper.

2 Put the salmon on this, adding seasoning and a squeeze of lemon juice.

3 Tie the paper round the salmon, making a neat parcel.

4 Put into a pan of cold water, with a little oil or butter and lemon juice in the water (vinegar could be used instead).

5 Bring steadily to the boil.

6 With a very small piece of salmon, remove from the heat at once.

7 Put a lid on the pan and allow the fish to cool in the liquid.

8 If cooking a larger piece of salmon, continue to simmer gently, allowing 10 minutes per lb. When cooked, allow the salmon to stand in the water for a short time, then lift out, and unwrap.

Skate with cream sauce

cooking time: 15 minutes

you will need:

4 portions of skate	2 teaspoons chopped
1 oz. butter	chives or spring
1 oz. flour	onions
½ pint milk	parsley
2 tablespoons cream	½ teaspoon grated
hard-boiled egg	lemon rind
	little lemon juice

stock for cooking fish:

seasoning	onion
parsley	water

1 Put skate into cold salted water.

2 Bring to boil and skim.

3 Add sprig of parsley and onion.

4 Simmer for just 10 minutes.

5 Meanwhile, make sauce of butter, flour and milk.

6 Add cream, chopped hard-boiled egg and other ingredients.

7 Strain fish and put on to hot dish.

8 Cover with sauce.

9 Serve with creamed or new potatoes and young carrots.

Variation:

Fish pie – follow the recipe for Skate with cream sauce, but cook any white fish you like. Put the fish and sauce into a pie dish, top with creamy mashed potato and bake.

Mock lobster salad

cooking time: 10 minutes

you will need:

approximately	2–3 drops anchovy
1½ lb. skate	essence (optional)
mayonnaise	lettuce
little tomato ketchup	tomatoes
	radishes, etc.

1 Boil fish as in recipe for skate with cream sauce making certain you do not overcook fish.
2 Blend a little tomato ketchup (or purée) into mayonnaise to give a faint pink colour.
3 Add anchovy essence if wished.
4 Coat flaked fish with mixture.
5 Serve on a bed of lettuce garnished with tomatoes, radishes, etc.

Variation:

Italian fish salad – recipe as above, using any white fish, but cook this in seasoned white wine at stage 1 instead of water and cook until tender. Use any white wine left over instead of tomato purée to add to the mayonnaise stage 2. Serve garnished with olives, green pepper and tomatoes.

Table for baking fish

Baking fish is a simple and tasty way of cooking it, but DO NOT overcook, as so much of the flavour will be lost. Correct times and oven temperatures for baking fish are given below.

Type of fish	Cooking time
Fillets, thin	approximately 15 minutes in moderate to moderately hot oven (375°F.–400°F. – Gas Mark 4–5)
Thicker cutlets	approximately 20–25 minutes, oven temperatures as above
Whole fish: Herrings	25 minutes
Codling, Haddock etc.	up to 40 minutes, oven temperatures as above

Plaice with mushroom cheese sauce

cooking time: 15–20 minutes

you will need:

8 fillets plaice
salt and pepper
1 oz. butter
juice ½ small lemon
1 can condensed cream of mushroom soup

¼ can liquid (made from fish stock and water)
3 oz. grated cheese
pinch pepper

to garnish:
paprika pepper

parsley

1 Season each fillet and roll into a curl.
2 Place in a well-buttered fireproof dish, and sprinkle with lemon juice.
3 Cover and bake in a moderate oven (375°F. – Gas Mark 4) for 15–20 minutes.
4 To make the sauce, empty the mushroom soup into a saucepan, add stock and mix well. Heat thoroughly.
5 Add cheese and pepper, and coat fish.
6 Decorate with a thin line of paprika pepper and a sprig of parsley.

Fish mornay

cooking time: 20 minutes

you will need:

4 fillets white fish (filleted sole, plaice, whiting—or, for economy, fillets fresh haddock or cod)

½ pint cheese sauce (see page 88)
little extra butter

to garnish: lemon and parsley

1 Either bake the fish in a little of the milk and butter from sauce and seasoning, until tender, or grill it.
2 Make the sauce, adding the stock from the fish at the last minute.
3 Arrange the fillets of fish on a dish.
4 Pour over the sauce and garnish with lemon and parsley.

Stuffed cod or haddock with mushroom stuffing

cooking time: 30–35 minutes

you will need:
1 fish weighing about 2½ lb.

for stuffing:
4 oz. mushrooms
1 oz. butter or margarine
2 teaspoons chopped parsley
grated rind 1 lemon

1 dessertspoon lemon juice
1 egg
4 oz. breadcrumbs
seasoning

to serve:
½ pint white, parsley or cheese sauce (see page 88)

few extra mushrooms

1 Remove head from fish.
2 Split it down the under-side (or get the fishmonger to do this for you).
3 Chop the mushrooms for the stuffing and mix with all the other ingredients. *continued*

4 Press into fish and tie or skewer into position.

5 Put into a greased dish, cover with greased paper.

6 Bake for approximately 30 minutes in the centre of a moderate oven (375°F. – Gas Mark 4) DO NOT OVERCOOK.

7 Test, and if fish is just coming away from skin it is cooked.

8 Lift on to a hot dish and garnish with grilled or fried mushrooms.

9 Serve with the hot sauce and fried potatoes, green peas or cauliflower.

Stuffed mackerel with paprika sauce

cooking time: 20 minutes

you will need:
4 medium sized
  mackerel

for stuffing:

2 oz. mushrooms	1 large skinned and
2 oz. breadcrumbs	chopped tomato
2 teaspoons suet,	few drops lemon juice
margarine or butter	seasoning

for sauce:

1 oz. margarine or	salt
butter	2 level teaspoons
1 oz. flour	paprika pepper
½ pint milk	

1 Split the mackerel and take out the backbone.

2 Make the stuffing by mixing the finely chopped mushrooms, with the other ingredients, lemon juice and seasoning.

3 Put into the mackerel and secure with small cocktail sticks.

4 Bake in a well greased dish covered with greased paper for 15 minutes in centre of a moderate oven (375°F. – Gas Mark 4). If the fish are fairly large, they will take 20 minutes.

5 While the fish is cooking, prepare the sauce. Heat margarine in a saucepan.

6 Stir in the flour and cook for 3 minutes.

7 Remove pan from heat and gradually add cold milk.

8 Bring gently to the boil, stirring all the time, until the sauce thickens.

9 Add a little salt and paprika pepper, whisking to make sure it is thoroughly mixed.

10 Serve with the fish.

Note: Paprika is an acquired taste so if uncertain whether it will be liked cut down the quantity – but it is surprisingly mild.

Lenten fish pudding

cooking time: 3 hours

you will need:
for suet crust:

8 oz. plain flour	pinch pepper
2 level teaspoons	4 oz. finely shredded
baking powder	suet
½ teaspoon salt	cold water to mix

for filling:

1 oz. margarine	salt and pepper
1 oz. flour	2 tablespoons chopped
¾ pint milk	parsley
1 lb. cooked flaked cod	little grated nutmeg

1 Well grease an 8-inch pudding basin.

2 Sieve plain flour, baking powder, salt and pepper.

3 Rub in suet lightly and mix to a light and spongy dough with cold water.

4 Turn on to floured board, cut off ⅔ of pastry, roll out to a round about ½ inch thick, dust with flour, fold in two and gather top edges to form a bag, slip into pudding basin and work into place.

5 Melt fat, add flour and cook without browning.

6 Slowly add milk to form a smooth sauce.

7 Add fish, seasoning, parsley and nutmeg, pour into lined basin.

8 Roll out remaining pastry to ½ inch thickness and cover right over rim of basin, pressing well round edges.

9 Trim the edge, cover with greaseproof paper and a pudding cloth.

10 Boil or steam for 3 hours.

Variation:

Fish and vegetable pudding – follow recipe above, but put 2 thinly sliced cooked carrots and 2 chopped raw onions into the sauce at stage 7.

Picnic pasty

cooking time: 40–45 minutes

you will need:

1 can condensed	1 teaspoon chopped
green pea soup	parsley
8 oz. cooked cod **or**	salt and pepper
4 hard-boiled eggs	8 oz. short crust
3 tablespoons mashed	pastry (see page **75**)
potato	little milk

1 Empty green pea soup into a pan.

2 Flake the fish and add to the soup (or chopped hard-boiled eggs).

3 Add potato, parsley and seasoning, and heat thoroughly.

4 Roll out pastry on a floured board in a large round about 9 inches in diameter.

5 Place soup mixture on to one half of the pastry.
6 Brush round the edge with milk, fold pastry over, seal edges and brush with milk.
7 Place on a greased baking sheet and bake in a moderately hot oven (400°F. – Gas Mark 5) for 40–45 minutes.

Variation:

Harvest pasty – use condensed mushroom soup instead of green pea soup; add 1 tablespoon chopped chives in addition to ingredients listed.

Lobster vol-au-vent

cooking time: 25–30 minutes

you will need:

8 oz. puff pastry (see page 76)	little cream
egg or milk to glaze	seasoning
1 medium sized lobster	lemon to garnish

for sauce:

1 oz. butter	⅓ pint milk
1 oz. flour	

1 Roll out the pastry to make a large circle or oval.
2 Make a smaller circle or oval in the centre pressing half-way through the pastry.
3 Brush the top with a little milk or egg if possible.
4 Bake for a good 10 minutes in the centre of a very hot oven (475°F. – Gas Mark 8).
5 Lower the heat for a further 10–15 minutes until the pastry is crisp and golden brown.
6 Meanwhile, make a sauce with the butter, flour and milk.
7 Remove pastry from the oven and with the tip of a sharp knife, remove the middle circle of pastry.
8 Return to the oven for a few minutes to dry out.
9 Flake the lobster meat and add to the sauce, together with the cream and seasoning.
10 Put hot filling into the hot pastry case and garnish with lemon, small lobster claws.
11 If serving cold, make sure that both pastry and filling are cold before they go together.

Shrimp or prawn mould

cooking time: 1 hour 10 minutes

you will need:

1 lb. cooked white fish	½ pint white sauce (see page 88)
½ pint shelled shrimps or prawns	2 eggs
	seasoning

1 Chop fish and shrimps – mix with sauce, egg yolks and seasoning.

2 Fold in stiffly-beaten egg whites.
3 Put into buttered mould (choose fancy shape if possible).
4 Cover with buttered paper.
5 Either steam for 1 hour or stand in dish of water and cook in very moderate oven for 1 hour.
6 Turn out and serve hot with parsley or hard-boiled egg sauce, and garnish with mixed vegetables.
7 OR serve cold with mayonnaise, which can be delicately flavoured with anchovy, or tomato or horseradish cream. Garnish with lettuce, tomatoes, cucumber.

Fisherman's pie

cooking time: 40 minutes

you will need:

1–1¼ lb. cooked white fish	seasoning
2 onions – boiled and chopped	1 lb. mashed potatoes
½–¾ pint white sauce (see page 88)	little margarine
	grated cheese
	few prawns or shrimps

1 Mix flaked fish and onions into sauce.
2 Season and put into dish
3 Cover with lattice work of piped potatoes.
4 Brush with melted margarine and cover with grated cheese.
5 Bake for 25–30 minutes in moderately hot oven (400°F. – Gas Mark 5).
6 Garnish with the prawns and shrimps.

Fish medley flan

cooking time: 25 minutes

you will need:

6 oz. short crust pastry (see page 75)	about ¼ pint thick white sauce (see page 88)
2 large tomatoes	3 tablespoons mayonnaise
seasoning	
about 8 oz. cooked fish or use canned tuna or salmon	1 can anchovy fillets
	few shrimps or prawns
	2 hard-boiled eggs
	parsley

1 Bake pastry 'blind' in a flan tin until golden in colour.
2 Arrange the sliced and seasoned tomatoes over the bottom of the flan.
3 Flake the fish and blend with the sauce, mayonnaise and half the chopped anchovy fillets and prawns.
4 Add 1 of the chopped hard-boiled eggs.
5 Spread over the sliced tomatoes, and top with

remaining anchovy fillets, prawns, chopped hard-boiled egg and parsley.

Variation:
Economy fish flan – omit the anchovy fillets and shrimps or prawns from the recipe before, and used diced cooked carrots, cooked peas and diced cooked potatoes instead.

Casserole dishes with fish

This method of cooking fish, is perhaps less usual than grilling, frying etc.; however, you should try it as it does result in a dish with a great deal of flavour.

Often it is not necessary to make a sauce, since the ingredients cooked with the fish provide their own liquid.

Here is one very simple way of making a **casserole dish with white fish:**

1 Put fish into buttered casserole.
2 Pour over a good flavoured soup – such as asparagus, cream of tomato, mushroom, etc.
3 Cover with foil or a lid and cook until the fish is tender.

Cod steaks with celery and bacon

cooking time: 35–40 minutes

you will need:

3 or 4 cod steaks (approximately 1 inch thick)	little milk
	1 oz. butter or margarine
1 small head celery	1½ level tablespoons flour
4 oz. streaky bacon	salt and pepper
1 teaspoon chopped parsley	

1 Sprinkle fish steaks with salt and leave for 30 minutes.
2 Wash and chop celery and cook in boiling salted water until tender.
3 Strain, saving stock.
4 Dice and fry bacon lightly.
5 Arrange the fish steaks in a greased ovenproof casserole dish and add any fish liquid to the celery stock.
6 Mix bacon, celery, parsley and pile on to the cod steaks.
7 Cover with lid or greased paper and bake in a moderate oven (375°F. – Gas Mark 4) for 35 minutes.
8 Add milk to the celery liquid to give ½ pint.

9 Make a sauce of the butter, flour, pepper and liquid.
10 Pour over fish and serve.

Variation:
Spanish cod – use 1 green pepper and 1 red pepper instead of celery, cut the peppers into rings and cook at stage 2 until tender. Flavour the sauce with garlic salt at stage 9.

Cod casserole

cooking time: 30–35 minutes

you will need:

1½ lb. cod fillets	½ pint milk
1 small onion	1 tablespoon chopped parsley
1–2 cloves (optional)	
1 bay leaf	2 oz. cheese
salt and pepper	2 hard-boiled eggs
2 oz. margarine	3 tomatoes
2 oz. flour	little parsley **for** garnish

1 Put fish in pan with onion stuck with cloves, bay leaf and salt.
2 Cover with water and cook gently until tender.
3 Remove fish, extract any skin or bones, and cut into large pieces.
4 Melt fat in pan, stir in the flour and add milk and strained fish liquor to make a smooth sauce.
5 Add parsley, grated cheese, chopped hard-boiled egg and seasoning.
6 Grease a deep casserole.
7 Arrange alternate layers of fish and sauce, ending with a layer of sauce.
8 Decorate the top with quartered tomatoes and bake in a hot oven (425°F.–450°F. – Gas Mark 6–7) for 10–15 minutes.
9 Garnish with finely chopped parsley.

Haddock and mushroom casserole

cooking time: 40 minutes

you will need:
4 pieces fresh haddock   seasoning

for the mushroom stuffing:

2 oz. margarine	2 teaspoons chopped parsley
1 small onion	
4 oz. mushrooms	seasoning
8 tablespoons soft breadcrumbs	

1 First make stuffing. Heat margarine and fry very finely chopped onion in this.

2 Add finely chopped mushrooms (stalks as well), crumbs, parsley, seasoning.
3 Work together then press this on top of each piece of fish.
4 If you like a sauce, pour a little milk in the casserole.
5 Cover with a lid and bake for 40 minutes in moderate oven (375°F. – Gas Mark 4).
6 Use the milk to make a white or parsley sauce (see page 88). A cheese sauce also blends well with this dish (see page 88).

Variation:

Haddock and anchovy casserole – omit the mushrooms from the stuffing and use a can of anchovies instead, chop finely and add to the crumbs etc. Use the oil from the can and omit 1 oz. margarine.

Cod and onion Portugaise

cooking time: 1 hour

you will need:

4 portions of cod (fillet or steaks)	2 large onions
seasoning	¼ pint cider
4 medium sized tomatoes	2 teaspoons chopped parsley

for topping:

2 tablespoons grated cheese	2–3 tablespoons soft breadcrumbs
	1 oz. margarine

to garnish:

parsley	lemon

1 Put seasoned cod into casserole.
2 Skin and slice tomatoes thickly, but slice onions very thinly.
3 Put cider into dish, then add onions, parsley and finally tomatoes.
4 Cover casserole with lid and cook for 1 hour in a very moderate oven (350°F. – Gas Mark 3).
5 Lift off lid and put cheese, crumbs and margarine on top.
6 Brown for a few minutes under a grill.
7 Garnish with lemon and parsley.

Cod Creole

cooking time: 50 minutes

you will need:

1 lb. filleted cod	juice 1 lemon
salt and pepper	1 oz. butter

for sauce:

1 oz. butter	pinch mixed spice
1 oz. flour	½ teaspoon chilli sauce
¾ pint fish stock, or water with few drops anchovy essence	4 tomatoes
3 cloves	parsley

to garnish:

paprika pepper	strips of red or green pepper

1 Lay the fillets in a greased casserole, season and sprinkle with lemon juice.
2 Dab 1 oz. butter on top, cover loosely with greased paper and bake slowly for 30 minutes.
3 Melt the butter in a pan, sprinkle in the flour and blend well.
4 Add fish stock, cook until smooth sauce.
5 Add cloves, spice and chilli sauce.
6 Peel and chop the tomatoes, and add them with the parsley.
7 Simmer for about 20 minutes.
8 When ready, pour over the fish, cover loosely again, and continue to bake in moderate oven for about 20 minutes.
9 Just before serving, sprinkle lightly with paprika pepper to add colour, and garnish with strips of red or green peppers.

Tomato and haddock casserole

cooking time: 30 minutes

you will need:

2 onions	seasoning
3 oz. butter	1½–2 lb. fresh haddock
2 tablespoons parsley	4 oz. breadcrumbs
6 good-sized tomatoes	

1 Chop the onions very finely.
2 Spread some butter at the bottom of the dish.
3 Cover with half the chopped onion, parsley and sliced tomatoes. Season.
4 Arrange the fish, cut into convenient-sized pieces, on the tomatoes.
5 Cover with a layer of the remaining tomatoes, onion and parsley. Season.
6 Put crumbs over the top with rest of butter.
7 Cover with greased paper or foil.
8 Bake for approximately 25–30 minutes in the centre of a moderately hot oven (400°F. – Gas Mark 5).

Meat Dishes

Roasting meats

In the tables which follow, you will find instructions for the proper methods of roasting the most popular types and cuts of meat. However, it is also possible to roast some of the cheaper joints, providing you use a very LOW temperature, and allow at least twice to three times the normal period per lb.

There is also the question of the amount of fat to be used when roasting. During the past few years a great deal of emphasis has been placed on the fact that using a lot of fat is neither good nor necessary. Only a minimum amount is required to roast successfully, and in some cases none at all. The following tables indicate the amount necessary for different types of meat.

Tables for roasting meat

Beef

Do not put too much fat on beef since it will harden the outside of the roast. If cooking a sirloin cut in a covered roaster, or in foil, you will need no fat at all, and only a little fat is required for very lean pieces like topside.

Cut to choose Sirloin, Ribs, Fillet, Aitch-bone (good quality), Topside, Rump.

Cooking time 15 minutes per lb. plus 15 minutes over.

Well done: 20 minutes per lb., plus 20 minutes over, **or** 40 minutes per lb. in very slow oven.

Mutton or lamb

Lamb should be roasted with a small amount of fat. Mutton however, does not require any extra as there is generally a fair amount of fat on the joint.

Cut to choose Leg, Loin, Best end of neck (lamb), Shoulder, Breast, stuffed and rolled.

Cooking time 20 minutes per lb. plus 20 minutes over.

Pork

Do not put fat on pork when roasting, but to produce a crisp crackling, rub the skin with a little oil and sprinkle lightly with salt.

Cut to choose Loin, Leg, Bladebone, Spare rib.

Cooking time 25 minutes per lb. plus 25 minutes over.

Veal

Since this meat is very lean, it must have fat with it when being cooked, unless it is wrapped in greased paper or foil. Otherwise cover the top of the joint with a little fat and baste during cooking.

For a large joint, buy very fat bacon, and cut this into narrow strips. Insert these into a larding needle (a large carpet needle can be purchased, if the former is not available) and thread the strips through the joint. In this way, the meat will be kept tender and moist as it cooks.

Cut to choose Shoulder, Breast, Best end of neck, Loin, Fillet, Chump end of loin.

Cooking time 25 minutes per lb. plus 25 minutes over.

To make gravy for roast meat

cooking time: 5–10 minutes

1 When the meat has been roasted, lift on to a hot dish.
2 Pour away the surplus fat from the tin, leaving a good tablespoon, blend this with a little stock or water flavoured with a bouillon cube or gravy flavouring.
3 Bring to the boil.

Note: This makes a THIN gravy which is correct for a joint that is not stuffed.

For a THICK gravy, a good tablespoon of flour should be added to the fat and cooked for 2–3 minutes before adding stock.

Pot roast pork and cabbage

cooking time: 2 hours

you will need:

1 oz. butter	seasoning
2 large onions	pinch sage
2 lb. pork (take this from leg or loin)	1 good sized cabbage

1 Heat the butter and toss the thinly sliced onions in this.
2 Add the joint of pork and cook steadily in the pan until golden brown on all sides.
3 Add seasoning, sage and just about ¼ pint water.
4 Put a tightly fitting lid on the pan (or foil or greaseproof paper under the lid) and cook over a slow heat for about 1¼–1½ hours.
5 If worried about the water evaporating completely, you can lift lid and add more, but it should be just the right amount.
6 Add the finely shredded cabbage, toss in the fat and liquid at the bottom of the pan.
7 Continue cooking for a further 30 minutes until the cabbage is tender and the pork cooked.
8 Drain the cabbage from the liquid in the pan.
9 Arrange with the onion on a hot dish with the pork in the centre.
10 Use the fat, etc., at the bottom of the pan for gravy.
11 Serve with mashed turnips and boiled potatoes.

Variation :

Pot roast beef and vegetables – use the same method as for pork, but use a rolled piece of beef instead. Use water as in the recipe for pork or use red wine, at stage 3. Instead of cabbage at stage 6, add sliced potatoes and carrots.

Rolled pork

cooking time: 2½ hours

you will need :
3 lb. piece of pork belly

for stuffing :

2 oz. slice of bread, diced	½ teaspoon chopped thyme
1 oz. seedless raisins	8 oz. pork sausage meat
1 stick celery or chicory	salt and pepper
1 small chopped onion	1 beaten egg

1 Bone and flatten the pork.
2 Mix together all the stuffing ingredients, spread over the pork, roll up and tie securely.
3 Place the bones on top.
4 Bake in an open roasting tin in a very moderate oven (350°F. – Gas Mark 3) for 2½ hours.

Stuffed breast of lamb

cooking time: 1¼ hours

Breast of lamb is very economical to buy, although many people dislike the fact that it is rather fat. If, however, you use a stuffing that absorbs some of the fat content, it will be a great help and the flavour of the meat is excellent. If boning and rolling, ask the butcher to remove the bones. They can be used as a base for stock when making soup or gravy. This stuffing is economical and very good.

you will need :
1 good-sized breast of lamb

for stuffing :

8 tablespoons breadcrumbs	1 tomato
1 oz. rolled oats	1 egg
2 large onions	little chopped parsley
	seasoning

1 Mix all the ingredients together. The onion should be chopped very finely and the tomato skinned and chopped.
2 Spread over the lamb and roll firmly.
3 Roast for approximately 1–1¼ hours in a moderately hot oven (400°F. – Gas Mark 5).

To vary:
Instead of the stuffing above try:

Sausagemeat and kidney – blend about 12 oz. sausagemeat with 1–2 chopped lamb's kidneys, good pinch sage and seasoning.

Sage and apricot – use a packet of sage and onion stuffing instead of breadcrumbs in the recipe and add about 4 oz. chopped canned apricots instead of the onions and tomato, bind with the egg, parsley, seasoning and a little apricot juice.

Roast stuffed breast of lamb

cooking time: depending on size of joint

you will need :

1 breast lamb (boned)	1 oz. dripping or lard

for stuffing :

8 oz. sausagemeat	salt and pepper
1 small onion, chopped	2 oz. fresh bread-crumbs
1 dessertspoon chopped parsley	

1 Wipe the meat with a damp cloth.
2 Trim away any excess fat.
3 Mix together the sausagemeat, onion, parsley, seasoning and breadcrumbs.
4 Spread the stuffing on the meat.
5 Roll up loosely and tie securely with string.
6 Place in a roasting tin with the dripping.
7 Roast in a moderate oven (375°F. – Gas Mark 4) allowing 40–45 minutes per pound.

Gourmet-style roast leg of lamb

cooking time: depending on size of joint

you will need:

1 leg lamb	1 oz. dripping or lard
1 clove garlic	¼ pint orange juice
cooking oil	3 tablespoons
salt and pepper	demerara sugar
2 tablespoons flour	

1 Wipe the joint with a damp cloth.
2 Rub the joint with a cut clove of garlic then make small incisions in the skin of the joint and insert slivers of garlic.
3 Brush the skin over with oil, then dust with seasoned flour.
4 Place the joint in a roasting tin with the dripping and roast in a moderate oven (350°F. – Gas Mark 3) allowing 25–30 minutes per pound.
5 When half cooked, sprinkle the meat with half the orange juice.
6 Repeat ten minutes later, then ten minutes before the end of the cooking time sprinkle the meat with sugar.
7 Remove garlic before serving.

Variations

Pineapple glazed lamb – use canned pineapple juice with a little fresh lemon juice instead of orange juice.

Tomato glazed lamb – use canned or bottled tomato juice instead of orange juice and only 1 tablespoon sugar.

Crown roast

cooking time: approximately 1¼–1½ hours

you will need:

loin of lamb 4–4½ lb. shaped into a crown (the butcher will do this for you)

for stuffing:

2 oz. dried apricots	1½ oz. nuts
3 oz. prunes	grated rind and juice
4 oz. breadcrumbs	½ lemon
1 cooking apple	1 tablespoon oil

for gravy:

¼ oz. cornflour	seasoning
½ pint stock	

to garnish:

1 small can halved apricots	8–10 cherries parsley

1 Soak apricots and prunes overnight.
2 Protect the tip of each rib bone with foil or greaseproof paper.

3 Brush the whole of the loin with a little oil.
4 Mix all the ingredients for the stuffing together and bind with the lemon juice and oil.
5 Place in the centre of the loin and cook for 1¼–1½ hours in a moderately hot oven (400°F. – Gas Mark 5).
6 When cooked, remove the foil or greaseproof paper.
7 Place the crown roast in a serving dish and keep warm while making gravy.
8 Drain any excess oil from the roasting tin, leaving about a dessertspoon.
9 Add the cornflour and cook for 1 minute.
10 Add the stock, bring to the boil and boil for 3 minutes stirring all the time.
11 Season to taste.
12 To serve, place a cutlet frill on each rib, and garnish the crown roast with apricots, cherries and parsley.
13 Serve the gravy separately.

Mint-glazed shoulder of lamb

cooking time: depending on size of joint

you will need:

1 shoulder lamb	3 tablespoons honey
salt and pepper	1 tablespoon chopped
1 oz. dripping or lard	mint

1 Season joint with salt and pepper and place in a roasting tin with the dripping.
2 Roast in a moderate oven (375°F. – Gas Mark 4) allowing 25–30 minutes per pound (or as given in table, page 22).
3 Mix the honey and mint together.
4 30 minutes before the end of cooking time, remove the joint from the oven and coat with the honey mixture.
5 Return to the oven to finish cooking.

Gammon steak and pineapple

cooking time: 30 minutes

you will need:

4 thick slices gammon 1 inch thick	little oil
	1 level teaspoon dry mustard
1 small can pineapple slices	1 level teaspoon cornflour
4 cloves	

1 Trim the rind from the gammon and arrange 4 slices pineapple on top.
2 Spike the gammon fat with the cloves.
3 Brush with oil, sprinkle with mustard and cornflour, then place in an ovenproof dish.

4 Pour over the pineapple juice from the can.

5 Bake for 20–30 minutes in a moderately hot oven (400°F. – Gas Mark 5).

6 When cooked, remove cloves and put gammon and pineapple on serving dish.

Variations:

With glazed apple rings – top with cored, but not skinned rings of dessert apple at stage 1 and use either apple or orange juice at stage 4.

With sweet sour onion rings – cover each gammon steak with several thin onion slices at stage 1. Add the ingredients as recipe above at stage 3, plus a good sprinkling of brown sugar. Spoon over tomato juice at stage 4 instead of pineapple juice.

Roast stuffed shoulder of lamb

cooking time: depending on size of joint

you will need:
shoulder of lamb

for stuffing:

1 good-sized onion	6 tablespoons soft
2 rashers bacon (or	breadcrumbs
2 oz. bacon fat)	seasoning
chopped celery or use	1 tablespoon chopped
diced raw potato and	parsley
add ½ teaspoon	good sized grated
celery salt)	carrot

1 Ask the butcher to bone the shoulder and use the bone for stock. Wipe meat, sprinkle salt and pepper into 'pocket' where the bone was.

2 Fry finely chopped onion with chopped bacon or bacon fat.

3 Add all other ingredients.

4 Mix well and press into pocket of the meat.

5 Roast and serve with braised onions.

Stuffed lamb roll

cooking time: 2 hours

you will need:
1 large piece middle neck of lamb or 2 small pieces per person (your butcher will cut these for you)
mixed vegetables

for stuffing:

1½ teacups bread-	1 tomato
crumbs	1 egg
1 oz. rolled oats	little chopped parsley
2 large onions	seasoning

1 Mix all stuffing ingredients together; the onion

should be chopped very finely and the tomato skinned and chopped.

2 Press a little of the stuffing on to each piece of meat.

3 Put into a dish on a bed of finely sliced vegetables.

4 Cover with foil or buttered paper and cook for about 2 hours very slowly at 300–325°F. – Gas Mark 2.

Stuffed leg of lamb with spring vegetables

cooking time: depending on weight of lamb

you will need:
good-sized leg of lamb

for stuffing:

8 oz. breadcrumbs	little chopped mint or
4 oz. rather fat bacon	parsley
2 oz. chopped	egg
mushrooms	seasoning
1 large finely chopped	
onion	

for serving:

young carrots	small onions
parsley, chopped	tomatoes
turnips	roast potatoes
nutmeg	

1 Either get your butcher to bone the leg, or slit it down the side.

2 Mix the crumbs with the finely chopped bacon, mushrooms, onion, mint and egg.

3 Season well and press into the slit or cavity where the bone was.

4 Tie securely.

5 Roast in the usual way (see page 22).

6 Serve with whole carrots tossed in butter and chopped parsley, small turnips or mashed turnips formed into pyramid shapes and dusted with a little nutmeg, and boiled onion, baked tomatoes and roast potatoes.

Stuffed shoulder of lamb

cooking time: depending on size of joint

you will need:
1 shoulder lamb (boned)

for mushroom stuffing:

8 oz. mushrooms	salt and pepper
1 small onion	1 teaspoon Worcester-
2 oz. dripping or lard	shire sauce
4 oz. fresh bread-	1 egg
crumbs	
1 tablespoon chopped	
parsley	

1 Wipe the joint with a damp cloth. *continued*

2 Prepare and chop the mushrooms and onion.
3 Sauté in 1 oz. of the dripping until tender.
4 Add the breadcrumbs, parsley, seasoning and Worcestershire sauce.
5 Bind together with beaten egg.
6 Stuff the joint with this mixture, then roll up and tie securely with string.
7 Place in a roasting tin with the remaining 1 oz. of dripping and roast in a moderate oven (375°F. – Gas Mark 4) allowing 35–40 minutes per pound, or as in tables, page 22.

Roast veal with creamed sauce

cooking time: 1 hour 40 minutes

you will need:

joint veal (approximately 3 lb.)	2 tablespoons cream
fat, bacon fat or butter for keeping moist	¾ pint rather thin white sauce (see page 88)
seasoning	

1 Season veal and cover with plenty of fat and paper or foil (or insert strips of fat through meat with 'larding' needle).
2 Allow 25 minutes per lb. and 25 minutes over in a moderately hot oven (400°F. – Gas Mark 5).
3 30 minutes before the end of cooking time, take joint out of oven.
4 Remove paper and pour off most of the fat from the tin, leaving about 1 tablespoon.
5 Blend cream with sauce, pour into meat tin.
6 Baste joint with this.
7 Continue cooking as before, but lower heat to moderate, basting several times with the sauce.
8 Serve with mixed vegetables.

Variations:

Roast veal with paprika sauce – blend 2 teaspoons paprika with the cream and the sauce at stage 5, and when heated add about 3 tablespoons tiny cocktail onions.

Devilled roast veal – follow directions for roast veal with creamed sauce but add 1 tablespoon Worcestershire sauce, 2 teaspoons made mustard and good shake cayenne pepper to the sauce and cream at stage 5.

Roast stuffed bacon

cooking time: 2 hours

you will need:

about 2½ lb. piece bacon (long back is ideal)	knob margarine or butter

for stuffing:

8 oz. sausage meat	1 small chopped onion
4 oz. breadcrumbs	1 tablespoon chopped parsley
grated rind 1 lemon	
1 teaspoon mixed herbs	1 egg

for the glaze:

1 teaspoon made mustard	2 tablespoons brown sugar
1 tablespoon lemon juice	1 tablespoon water

1 Soak bacon overnight, then dry.
2 Combine ingredients for stuffing, then spread on inner side of bacon and roll round.
3 Tie with string.
4 Put into covered roaster with little margarine or butter on the lean part of the bacon, or cover with buttered paper or foil.
5 Cook for 1½ hours in centre of moderately hot oven (400°F. – Gas Mark 5).
6 Take off lid or foil, remove rind of bacon.
7 Mix mustard, lemon juice, sugar and water.
8 Score the fat of the bacon and brush this glaze over it.
9 Continue cooking for a further 30 minutes.
10 Serve with baked apples or apple sauce, roast potatoes and a green vegetable.

Rice-stuffed roast cutlets

cooking time: 55 minutes

you will need:

4 cutlets	4 greaseproof paper bags or sheets of paper
extra butter for paper bags	

for stuffing:

2 oz. cooked rice	1 oz. butter or 1–2 rashers chopped bacon
1 tablespoon chopped parsley	
2 tablespoons chopped onion	egg
grated lemon rind	seasoning

1 Mix rice, parsley, onion, lemon rind, melted butter or chopped bacon together.
2 Add egg and seasoning.
3 Spread on top of each 4 cutlets.
4 Insert into 4 buttered bags, or wrap sheets of well buttered paper round cutlets.

5 Roast for approximately 35–45 minutes in moderately hot oven (400°F. – Gas Mark 5).

Variation:

Lemon raisin stuffed cutlets – use the recipe above, but add 3 oz. seedless raisins and the grated rind of 1 extra lemon to the rice at stage 1; use butter to blend.

Frying meat

Frying is a very popular way of cooking meat, and either a small amount of fat or deep fat can be used. Here are a few points to be kept in mind.

1 When SHALLOW FRYING always put the meat into HOT fat to seal the outside, then lower the heat for the remainder of the cooking time, in order to make sure it is cooked through to the centre.

2 Thick chops, steaks, etc. will need turning once or twice during cooking.

3 If you like a golden brown coating, you can either cover with well seasoned flour or coat with egg and crumbs. Fillets (i.e. slices) of veal or lamb cutlets, are often coated in this way.

4 DEEP FRYING methods are the same as for shallow frying. Make sure the fat is very hot before putting in the meat, then lower it at once to give the meat time to cook through to the centre.

5 When frying bacon, gammon, etc., you will find a better result is obtained if the meat is put into a cold pan. Unless frying very lean gammon, there is no need to add extra fat.

Parmesan cutlets

cooking time: 25 minutes

you will need:

8 small cutlets of lamb or mutton	approximately 1 oz. crisp breadcrumbs
1 egg	fat for frying
2 oz. grated Parmesan cheese	tomato sauce (see page 87)

1 Simmer the cutlets very gently for about 15 minutes in salted water or stock.

2 Drain and dry.

3 Coat with beaten egg and the cheese mixed with the crumbs.

4 Fry steadily until crisp and golden brown.

5 Drain and serve with tomato sauce, page 87, new or creamed potatoes and peas.

6 Garnish with cutlet frills.

Garnished lamb cutlets

cooking time: 15–20 minutes

you will need:

8 lamb cutlets	8 rashers streaky bacon
egg	4 lambs' kidneys
breadcrumbs	watercress
fat for frying	

1 Coat the cutlets in egg and breadcrumbs.

2 Fry gently in hot fat until tender.

3 Fry the bacon rashers.

4 Cut the kidneys in half and coat in egg and breadcrumbs.

5 Fry until golden.

6 Arrange the cutlets on a dish.

7 Cover with the bacon and top with the kidneys.

8 Garnish with sprigs of watercress.

Variations:

Lamb cutlets Portuguese – do not coat the cutlets, just fry until *nearly* tender. Lift on to a plate, then add a medium can tomatoes, 1–2 chopped or grated onions and a crushed clove garlic to the fat in the pan (pour out any surplus fat if wished). Heat well, then return the cutlets to this sauce and complete cooking.

Lamb cutlets in creamed mushroom sauce – do not coat the cutlets, fry until just tender. Keep hot, pour away all fat except about $\frac{1}{2}$ tablespoon, add 2–3 oz. thinly sliced mushrooms, $\frac{1}{4}$ pint thin cream, 3–4 tablespoons stock and seasoning. Simmer gently for 5 minutes then pour over the cutlets.

Peppered lamb cutlets – crush about 1 tablespoon peppercorns, press into both sides of the cutlets before frying; do not coat, just fry in fat until tender.

Luxury cutlets – do not coat the cutlets, fry in hot butter until nearly tender, then add 3 tablespoons dry sherry, 2 teaspoons chopped parsley, 2 oz. cooked ham (cut into thin strips). Heat with the meat for a few minutes then serve.

Cheese coated cutlets – fry the uncoated cutlets. Make a thick cheese mixture of 1 oz. butter, 1 oz. flour, $\frac{1}{4}$ pint milk, 3 oz. grated cheese, 2 oz. soft breadcrumbs and seasoning. Press on the cutlets then heat for a few minutes in the pan until the mixture starts to melt and serve at once.

Sausage-stuffed cutlets

cooking time: 20 minutes

you will need:
4 cutlets of lamb or mutton

for stuffing:

grated rind 1 lemon	1 egg
little chopped parsley	crumbs
8 oz. sausage meat	fat

1 Add grated lemon rind and parsley to sausage meat.
2 Press this over the top of each cutlet, keeping the shape intact.
3 Coat with beaten egg and crumbs.
4 Fry until crisp, brown and cooked.

Pork chop Milanaise

cooking time: 25–30 minutes

you will need:

2–3 oz. short-cut macaroni	1 onion
4 loin chops	3–4 tomatoes
seasoning	little stock
2 oz. margarine or butter	4 oz. breadcrumbs
	2–3 oz. grated cheese

1 Cook macaroni for approximately 7 minutes in boiling salted water.
2 Fry seasoned pork chops steadily in most of the hot butter or margarine.
3 When tender lift on to a hot dish and keep warm.
4 Fry the thinly sliced onion, then the tomatoes in the fat remaining in the pan, add a little stock.
5 When tender mix with the cooked and drained macaroni.
6 Arrange in a serving dish, topped with the pork chops, breadcrumbs and cheese and a little butter.
7 Brown under the grill. Serve with green salad.

Veal escalopes

cooking time: 10–15 minutes

you will need:

4 thin fillets veal	1 tablespoon chopped parsley
seasoning	
4 oz. butter	olives
juice 1 lemon	

1 Fry the seasoned fillets of veal in hot butter for about 4–5 minutes on either side.
2 Lift on to hot dish.
3 Cook butter left in pan with lemon juice until golden brown, add parsley.
4 Pour over meat. Garnish with olives.

Veal escalopes or fillets in cream sauce

cooking time: 15–20 minutes

you will need:

ingredients as before, plus ⅓ pint thin cream	mushrooms

1 Cook the fillets veal as before.
2 Lift on to hot dish.
3 Add cream to butter remaining in pan and cook steadily until golden brown.
4 Whisk in lemon juice (do not boil) and add parsley.
5 Pour over meat and garnish with fried mushrooms.

Veal and ham fritter with fried eggs

cooking time: 15 minutes

you will need:

8 oz. veal	pinch sage
8 oz. ham or boiled bacon	2 eggs
8 oz. breadcrumbs	fat for frying
1 tablespoon chopped onion	4 eggs

1 Mince veal and ham.
2 Mix with half breadcrumbs, onion and sage.
3 Bind with a beaten egg.
4 Form into 4 flat cakes.
5 Roll in the second egg and crumbs.
6 Fry steadily in hot fat.
7 Fry the 4 eggs and serve on top of the 4 cakes.

Variations:

Veal and ham rissoles – as before but use cooked veal instead of uncooked veal, and to prevent the fritters becoming too dry use only 2 oz. crumbs to bind. Cooking time: 10 minutes.

Beef and ham rissoles – use minced beef instead of veal and flavour with 1–2 teaspoons made mustard.

Fried ham

cooking time: 10 minutes

you will need:

sprinkling of flour	1 teaspoon made mustard
4 thick slices cooked ham	2 tablespoons water
2 oz. butter	little brown sugar

1 Flour the ham lightly.
2 Heat the butter and toss the ham in this until piping hot.
3 Lift on to hot dish.
4 Add mustard, water and sugar to fat remaining in pan.
5 Pour over ham and serve.
6 Delicious with mushrooms, fried potatoes and eggs.

Corned beef cutlets

cooking time: 15 minutes

you will need:

4 oz. breadcrumbs	1 egg
1 12-oz. can corned beef	crisp breadcrumbs fat for frying
seasoning	

for sauce:

1 oz. margarine	¼ pint milk or stock
1 oz. flour	

1 Make the sauce by heating the margarine in the pan, stirring the flour into the margarine and cooking for 2 minutes, then adding the liquid.
2 Bring to the boil and cook until thick.
3 Add the breadcrumbs and flaked corned beef.
4 Season well and form into cutlet shapes.
5 Coat with beaten egg and crisp breadcrumbs.
6 Fry in hot fat until crisp and golden brown.
7 Serve hot with fried tomatoes, peas and sauté potatoes or cold with salad.

Grilling meat

Many people prefer grilling meat to frying, particularly when cooking steaks. For successful grilling, keep in mind the following points:

1 Make sure the grill is hot before putting meat underneath.
2 Keep LEAN meat, such as steaks or fillets, well brushed with melted fat during the cooking process. Kidneys, liver etc. also need frequent brushing with fat, to prevent them from becoming too dry. Chops however, require very little.
3 Seal the outside of the meat under a high grill, then turn heat low to cook through to centre.
4 When grilling thick bacon rashers or slices of bacon or gammon DO NOT pre-heat the grill. Put the meat under the cold grill, then heat. This method prevents the fat from curling at the edges. Snip it with kitchen scissors to encourage it to become crisp.

Grilled lamb cutlets with Gruyère cheese

cooking time: 15–20 minutes

you will need:

8 small lamb cutlets	parsley
little butter	
4 slices Gruyère cheese	

1 Brush the lean part of the cutlets with a little melted butter.
2 Put on the grid on the grill pan and cook under the hot grill until brown and tender, turning as necessary.
3 Divide each slice of cheese in half then put on top of the cooked cutlets.
4 Put under the grill for a few minutes to melt the cheese.
5 Garnish with chopped parsley.

Grilled veal cutlets

cooking time: 15–20 minutes

you will need:

4 cutlets veal (cut from loin)	mushrooms tomatoes
little melted butter or margarine	watercress

1 Heat grill, brush cutlets with melted butter.
2 Cook steadily under the grill, standing meat on grid.
3 Cook mushrooms and tomatoes in grill pan at the same time.
4 Garnish with watercress.

Variations:

Veal cutlets au gratin – grill as above, and when cutlets are cooked roll in a mixture of crisp crumbs and grated cheese and brown under grill on either side. Delicious served with creamy onion sauce (see page 87).

Veal cutlets mornay – grill the cutlets as above, arrange on hot dish and coat with cheese sauce (see page 88). Garnish with asparagus tips.

Veal cutlets in lemon sauce – grill as above and, when cooked, top each cutlet with soured cream, blended with grated lemon rind. Heat for 1–2 minutes only under the grill.

Piquant veal cutlets – blend the butter, at stage 1, with 1 tablespoon chutney, 1 teaspoon chilli sauce and 1 teaspoon made mustard.

Grilled stuffed kidneys with rice

cooking time: 15–20 minutes

you will need:

8 medium sized kidneys	little melted butter
8 rashers streaky bacon	4 oz. rice

for stuffing:

1 thick slice bread (crust removed)	1 can condensed tomato soup
1 small onion	pepper

1 Crumble bread and mix with chopped onion and ¼ can tomato soup. Season well.
2 Halve and stuff each of the kidneys and wrap securely in a rasher of bacon.
3 Switch grill on to high, brush grill pan with a little butter, place on kidneys and brush with butter.
4 Grill for 15–20 minutes, turning once during cooking.
5 Cook the rice in boiling salted water until tender, drain and dry.
6 Serve kidneys on the cooked rice.
7 Heat remaining tomato soup and serve separately as a sauce.

Variation:

Mushroom stuffed kidneys – use mushroom soup instead of tomato. Serve with pickled walnuts, as well as remaining mushroom soup.

Grilled gammon and pineapple

cooking time: 15 minutes

you will need:

4 slices of gammon	4 pineapple rings
1–2 oz. butter	parsley
light sprinkling of sugar (if wished)	

1 Snip round the edges of the gammon, having removed the skin, at ½-inch intervals.
2 Arrange on the grid of the grill pan, brushing the lean with melted butter.
3 Put under the grill, and light, then cook steadily, turning after about 5 minutes.
4 After 10 minutes cooking, sprinkle the meat with a little sugar, then arrange pineapple rings under the grill with the bacon.
5 Brush the pineapple with butter and sprinkle with sugar then continue cooking until both gammon and pineapple are golden brown and tender.
6 Garnish with parsley.

Variation:

Grilled gammon and peaches – follow previous recipe, but use peaches instead of pineapple. Garnish with glacé cherries.

Grilled tournedos of steak

cooking time: 6–12 minutes

you will need:

4 steak tournedos	garnish (see below)
butter	

1 If the butcher has not made the fillets of steak into tournedos, you can do it yourself. Form them into neat rounds and tie them with fine string.
2 Heat the grill*, and brush the steaks liberally with melted butter, putting them on the greased grid of the grill pan.
3 Cook according to personal taste, allowing about 3 minutes on either side for underdone thick tournedos – up to about 6 minutes on either side for medium well done. For well done steaks, lower the heat slightly after the first few minutes.
4 Dish up the tournedos and garnish as below. The tournedos are generally served on crisp rounds of fried bread.

*The steaks can be fried in butter instead of grilled if wished.

Garnishes for tournedos:

Tournedos Africaine – serve with fried bananas and horseradish sauce.

Tournedos Dumas – cover cooked steak with onion sauce (see page 87) and grated cheese, then top with slices of ham and brown again under the grill. Serve with croquette potatoes.

Tournedos Othello – top with poached or fried egg.

Tournedos d'Orsay – top with olives and cooked mushrooms.

Variations:

Peppered steaks – either sprinkle both sides of the steak with black pepper or press crushed peppercorns against the meat before frying.

Steaks au poivre – this is a more elaborate version of the peppered steak above. Prepare and fry the peppered steaks, lift on to a hot dish, then add cream and brandy to the butter remaining in the pan. Heat and pour over the meat.

Steak Diane

Toss a finely chopped onion in about 3 oz. butter; flavour this with a little chopped parsley and Worcestershire sauce. Fry 3–4 very thin steaks in this mixture, lift out. Add a little brandy to the pan if wished, heat and pour over the meat and serve.

Baked meat dishes

The following recipes give a variety of baked meat dishes. The difference between baking and roasting is that in a baked dish, the meat is frequently pre-cooked, and then combined with other ingredients, as in Shepherd's pie. Or the meat may be cooked in with other ingredients in order to give it more flavour. This keeps it moist.

Beef Braemar

cooking time: 25 minutes

you will need:

2 sliced onions	8 tablespoons fresh
2 oz. butter	breadcrumbs
4–8 oz. mushrooms	4 oz. grated Cheddar
1 lb. diced roast beef	cheese
	salt and pepper

1 Fry the onions in butter until golden.
2 Then add the mushrooms, cook for 2 minutes.
3 Arrange the meat, onion and mushrooms in an ovenproof dish.
4 Sprinkle with the breadcrumbs.
5 Top with the cheese, add salt and pepper.
6 Pour any remaining fat over the top and bake in oven (450°F. – Gas Mark 7) for about 15 minutes.

Variation:

Highland lamb – use diced cooked lamb instead of beef and add a little chopped mint at stage 3.

Curried shepherd's pie (1) (with uncooked meat)

cooking time: 1¼ hours

you will need:

2 onions	12 oz. freshly minced
1 oz. fat	beef
½ oz. flour	seasoning
1 tablespoon curry	1 tablespoon chutney
powder	1 lb. mashed potatoes
½ pint stock* (or small	
can tomatoes and	
little stock)	

*less stock can be used if wished

1 Fry the onions (finely chopped) in the hot fat.
2 Add flour and curry powder.
3 Then add stock or tomatoes and stock.
4 Bring to the boil and cook until thickened.
5 Add the minced beef and cook gently stirring from time to time to 'break up' any lumps in the mince.
6 Add seasoning and chutney.
7 When the meat is tender, put into a pie dish.
8 Cover with the mashed potatoes (and little margarine and grated cheese if wished).
9 Brown in the oven until crisp.

Variations:

Curried shepherd's pie (2) (with cooked meat) – method as above, but at step 5 add the minced or diced cooked meat, heat for a few minutes only, then proceed with remainder of recipe. Cooking time approximately 30 minutes.

Tomato shepherd's pie – omit the curry powder in either of the two recipes and fry 3–4 skinned sliced tomatoes with the onions at stage 1. Use stock at stage 3.

Beef and tomato loaf

cooking time: 1¼ hours

you will need:

12 oz. tomatoes	seasoning
1½ lb. minced beef	1 tablespoon chopped
3 rashers bacon	parsley or chives
3 oz. rolled oats	

1 Skin tomatoes and chop coarsely.
2 Mix with beef, finely chopped bacon and other ingredients.
3 Put into well greased loaf tin, and cover with greased paper.
4 Bake in the centre of a very moderate oven (350°F. – Gas Mark 3) for 1½ hours.
5 Turn out after standing for 15–20 minutes.

Devilled lamb fillets

cooking time: 35 minutes

you will need:

4 slices lamb cut from	1 tablespoon Wor-
top of leg	cestershire sauce
seasoning	3 tablespoons water
2 oz. butter	3–4 pickled walnuts
1 teaspoon made	few pickled onions
mustard	

1 Fry the seasoned slices of lamb in the hot fat for a few minutes on either side. *continued*

2 Transfer to shallow dish.

3 Blend mustard and sauce with boiling water.

4 Pour over meat adding chopped walnuts and onions.

5 Cook for about 25 minutes in a moderately hot oven.

6 Serve with rice, chutney and green vegetables.

Kidney and lamb toad-in-the-hole

cooking time: 45 minutes

you will need:

4 small lamb chops or cutlets	4 small tomatoes
2 lamb's kidneys	knob fat

for batter:

4 oz. plain flour	1 egg
pinch salt	½ pint milk and water

1 Sieve flour and salt.

2 Gradually beat in egg, milk and water.

3 Put cutlets into good sized baking dish and cook for 10 minutes in a really hot oven.

4 Add halved kidneys, tomatoes and fat and heat for further 5 minutes.

5 Pour over batter and cook for 15–20 minutes until well risen.

6 Reduce heat slightly and cook for further 10–15 minutes.

Variation:

Sausage toad-in-the-hole – use about 1 lb. sausages at stage 3, instead of meat. Cook for 10 minutes if large sausages, 5 minutes if small; then proceed as recipe.

Veal and vegetable cottage pie

cooking time: 1 hour 35 minutes

you will need:

1 oz. flour	8 oz. diced root vegetables
approximately 1 lb. stewing veal	2 hard-boiled eggs
2 oz. dripping	1½ lb. mashed potatoes
stock or water with yeast extract	little margarine
seasoning	

1 Flour the diced veal well then fry in the hot dripping.

2 Add stock or water flavoured with yeast extract, to cover. Season.

3 Bring to the boil and cook until thickened.

4 Add vegetables and simmer gently for about 1¼ hours until the meat is tender.

5 Transfer to a pie dish – the mixture should be fairly stiff by this time – if not, spoon out some of the gravy, which can be served separately.

6 Cover the meat mixture with sliced hard-boiled eggs, then the potatoes.

7 Put knobs of margarine on top and brown for about 20 minutes in a moderately hot oven.

Savoury baked tripe

cooking time: 1 hour 40 minutes

you will need:

1 lb. dressed tripe	little chopped parsley
1 small onion	pinch herbs
2 eggs	seasoning
½ pint milk	

1 Blanch the tripe (see below).

2 Cut the onion into small pieces and the tripe into narrow fingers.

3 Simmer gently together for about 1 hour until tender.

4 Strain and keep about ½ pint of the stock.

5 Beat the eggs, add milk and tripe stock.

6 Put the tripe in a casserole.

7 Cover with egg mixture, parsley and herbs.

8 Season well.

9 Bake for about 40 minutes in the centre of a very moderate oven (325°F.–350°F. – Gas Mark 2–3), standing the dish in another of cold water.

To blanch tripe: put into cold salted water, bring to the boil. Throw water away and continue cooking as indicated in individual recipes.

Variation:

Creamed tripe – proceed as stages 1–4 in recipe above. Make a white sauce as page 88 with ½ pint milk etc. and 2–3 tablespoons cream. Stir the tripe and onions in this with ¼ pint tripe stock and season well. Heat and serve with crisp toast or creamed potatoes.

Tongue rolls

cooking time: 15–20 minutes

you will need:

4 large slices tongue or 8 smaller thinner slices	4 large rashers bacon

for filling:

2 oz. breadcrumbs	seasoning
2 tomatoes (chopped)	little chopped parsley
2 chopped gherkins	1 egg

1 Halve the large slices of tongue and halve the rashers of bacon.
2 Mix all the ingredients for the stuffing together.
3 Spread over the pieces of tongue.
4 Roll firmly, then wrap round in the bacon.
5 Put into 4 greaseproof paper bags or 3 pieces of paper or foil.
6 Bake for 15–20 minutes in a hot oven (450°F. – Gas Mark 7) until the bacon is cooked and the tongue is really hot.
7 Serve with mixed vegetables.

Variation:

Curried tongue rolls – use the filling above, but blend ½–1 teaspoon curry powder and a small grated onion with the ingredients. If wished, fry the onion and curry powder in ½ oz. margarine first, to give a softer texture to the filling.

Ham and beef galantine

cooking time: 1½ hours

you will need:

12 oz.–1 lb. minced beef	1 dessertspoon chopped chives
4 oz. chopped ham	3–4 oz. breadcrumbs
2 eggs	seasoning

to glaze:

3 tablespoons mayonnaise	tiny pieces of gherkin
¼ pint aspic jelly	tomato
	radish

1 Mix all ingredients together.
2 Place on greased tin or mould and cover top of tin with greased paper.
3 Either steam, or bake for approximately 1¼–1½ hours in a very moderate oven (350°F. – Gas Mark 3).
4 Turn out and cool.

To make glaze:

5 Stir the thick mayonnaise into the aspic jelly when cold.
6 Allow to stiffen slightly and coat the galantine.
7 Spread with knife dipped in hot water.
8 When firm, make a pattern of gherkin, tomato and radish.
9 Serve with salad platter of spring onions, halved tomatoes, sliced cucumber and potato salad.

Casseroles

Stewing meat in the oven

I have included a great variety of casserole dishes in this section because I think most people will agree that they are probably one of the easiest and most delicious ways of serving meat, poultry and even fish. And the great variety of attractive casseroles available today makes it possible to use the same dish for both cooking and serving.

When preparing a casserole, DO remember NOT to hurry things up by trying to cook it any more quickly than the recipe states. It is the long, slow cooking which produces the particularly pleasant flavour.

Beef and pepper ragoût

cooking time: 2¼ hours

you will need:

12 oz. potatoes	½ pint stock (or water and bouillon cube)
12 oz. chuck steak	3 tablespoons cheap red wine
12 oz. onions	
1 green pepper	3 large sliced tomatoes
2 oz. butter	salt and pepper
1 dessertspoon flour	breadcrumbs

1 Butter a large casserole dish and line with sliced potatoes.
2 Lay the chuck steak over this.   *continued*

3 Prepare a sauce by finely slicing onions and green pepper and browning in butter.
4 Stir in the flour and add stock.
5 Add the wine.
6 Pour the sauce over the meat and cover with sliced tomato. Season.
7 Sprinkle with breadcrumbs, dot with butter and cook in a very moderate oven (350°F. – Gas Mark 3) for 2 hours. Turn the heat up to 400°F. – Gas Mark 5 for the last 20 minutes to brown the breadcrumbs.

Variation:

Pork and apple ragoût – use the recipe above, but substitute about 1 lb. lean pork (cut from the leg) for beef and use 2–3 skinned sliced dessert apples and a sprinkling of sage instead of the pepper.

Tomato beef casserole

cooking time: 3 hours

you will need:

little butter	½ pint hot water
2–3 lb. topside beef	8 oz. spaghetti or
6 onions	macaroni
6 carrots	butter
1 lb. tomatoes (skinned)	grated cheese
2 meat extract cubes	

1 Melt butter in a saucepan or casserole.
2 Add beef, browning on all sides.
3 Add sliced onions, carrots, tomatoes, beef cubes dissolved in water.
4 Cover and cook either on top of the stove or in a slow oven (300°F. – Gas Mark 2) for 3 hours.
5 Cook spaghetti or macaroni in boiling salted water until tender; drain, toss in a little butter and add a little grated cheese.
6 Serve round the joint and vegetables.

Beef and corn stuffed marrow

cooking time: 1 hour

you will need:

1 medium sized marrow	1 lb. minced beef
3 tomatoes	1 heaped tablespoon flour
2 tablespoons oil or butter	½ pint of beef stock
1 finely chopped onion	seasoning
	1 can of corn

1 Wipe the marrow and scoop out the seeds.
2 Skin, chop and remove pips from tomatoes.
3 Melt oil or butter.
4 Add onion and fry gently.
5 Add mince and fry for 3–4 minutes.

6 Mix in the flour.
7 Add stock, seasoning and bring to the boil.
8 Simmer for 5 minutes.
9 Add corn and tomatoes and reseason if necessary.
10 Pile into marrow halves.
11 Place in a fireproof casserole and cover with a lid or foil.
12 Bake in a moderate oven (375°F. – Gas Mark 4) for 45 minutes or until cooked.
13 To serve, cut across the marrow into thick slices.

Spiced beef casserole

cooking time: 3 hours

you will need:

1–1½ lb. stewing beef	½ pint stock
1 oz. flour	1 clove garlic
½ teaspoon curry powder	(optional)
½ teaspoon paprika pepper	1 tablespoon Worcestershire sauce
½ teaspoon mixed spice	1 tablespoon vinegar
seasoning	8 small onions
2 oz. fat	6 oz. diced celery

1 Cut the meat into 1-inch squares.
2 Mix flavourings with the flour and roll meat in this.
3 Fry in a hot fat for a few minutes, then lift into casserole.
4 Add stock, garlic, sauce and vinegar to residue of fat and flour left in pan. Season.
5 Bring to boil and cook for several minutes.
6 Put onions and celery into casserole and cover meat and vegetables with the sauce.
7 Put on lid and cook for approximately 3 hours in a slow oven (300°F. – Gas Mark 3).

Countryman's bacon casserole

cooking time: 1¼ hours

you will need:

1½ lb. potatoes	seasoning
8 oz. onions	good pinch chopped sage
8 oz. cooking apples	1 oz. margarine
½–1 oz. sugar	
12 oz. lean cooked bacon	

1 Peel and slice the potatoes and onions very thinly.
2 Peel and slice the apples fairly thickly, sprinkle with sugar.
3 Cut the cooked bacon (this can either be fried rashers or boiled bacon) into neat pieces.

4 Put half the well-seasoned potatoes and onions at the bottom of the casserole.

5 Top with the apples, bacon and sage then the rest of the onions. Cover with the potatoes and the margarine.

6 Cook in the centre of a very moderate oven (325–350°F. – Gas Mark 3–4) for approximately 1¼ hours.

Variations:

With stock – the above recipe gives a fairly 'dry' texture; if wished add about ¼ pint stock.

Tomato bacon casserole – add a thick layer of sliced tomatoes instead of the apples.

Chuck steak and mushroom casserole

cooking time: 2 hours

you will need:

4 chuck steaks	4 oz. mushrooms
(4–6 oz. each)	1 beef extract cube
salt and pepper	¼ pint hot water
1 oz. flour	
8 oz. thinly sliced onion	

1 Ask your butcher for steaks cut 1 inch thick.

2 Roll the steak in seasoned flour.

3 Put the sliced onions and mushrooms into a casserole and place the steaks on top.

4 Dissolve the beef extract cube in hot water and pour over steaks.

5 Cover dish with foil or a well-fitting lid and cook in a slow oven (300°F. – Gas Mark 2) for 2 hours.

Lamb and butter bean casserole

cooking time: 3–4 hours

you will need:

1 small shoulder lamb	½ pint hot water
2 large onions	seasoning
2 oz. flour	1 large can butter
1 large can tomatoes	beans
1 beef extract cube	

1 Ask butcher to remove blade bone from shoulder and roll meat into neat shape.

2 Put with the sliced onions in ovenproof casserole.

3 Blend flour with can of tomatoes, add the beef cube dissolved in the hot water.

4 Pour over the onions in the casserole, season.

5 Cook in a slow oven (300°F. – Gas Mark 2) for 3–4 hours.

6 Ten minutes before serving, add drained butter beans.

Ragoût of pork

cooking time: approximately 1¼ hours

you will need:

1 beef extract cube	¾ oz. flour
½ pint hot water	salt and pepper
½ oz. lard	1 bay leaf
4 onions	1 small can tomato
4 pork chops	purée

1 Crumble and dissolve beef extract in hot water.

2 Melt the fat and cook the chopped onions for a few minutes.

3 Add the pork chops and brown on both sides.

4 Remove and stir the flour into the fat.

5 Add salt, pepper, bay leaf and tomato purée.

6 Replace the chops in the sauce and cook in a moderate oven (375°F. – Gas Mark 4) for 1 hour.

7 Remove the bay leaf and serve the chops with boiled potatoes.

American lamb casserole

cooking time: 2 hours 20 minutes

you will need:

8 scrag end lamb	clove garlic
chops	4 skinned tomatoes
seasoning	1–1½ lb. potatoes
little flour	about 3 tablespoons
fat or margarine	stock
2 large onions	

1 Fry the lamb chops, after coating with seasoned flour, for a few minutes, then lift out of pan.

2 If necessary, add little extra fat and fry thinly sliced onions, garlic and tomatoes for a few minutes.

3 Fill casserole with layers of meat, onions and tomatoes and thinly sliced potatoes, ending with potatoes.

4 Add seasoning and stock and put small amount of fat or margarine over top layer of potatoes.

5 Cover and cook for about 2 hours in a very moderate oven (350°F. – Gas Mark 3).

6 Take off lid and allow 15–20 minutes to brown potatoes.

Variation:

Minted lamb casserole – omit the tomatoes in the recipe above, but use 3 onions instead. When the onions and garlic have been fried at stage 2, sprinkle with a generous amount of freshly chopped mint. About 4 oz. uncooked peas could be added at stage 3.

Summer casserole

cooking time: 1½ hours

you will need:

2 lb. scrag end neck lamb	salt and pepper
fat for frying	2 sprigs mint
1 onion	1 sprig thyme
1 small turnip	4 oz. shelled peas (or
3 new carrots	1 small package
1 pint water	frozen peas)

1 Prepare the lamb and cut into pieces removing all gristle.
2 Fry meat in a little fat till lightly brown with finely chopped onion.
3 Drain and place the meat and onion in a casserole.
4 Dice the turnip and slice the carrot and add to the casserole with water.
5 Season with salt and pepper and add the mint and thyme.
6 Cover the casserole and place in a moderate oven (375°F. – Gas Mark 4) for about 1½ hours.
7 If fresh peas are used, cook them separately and stir into casserole just before serving.
8 If frozen peas are used, stir them into the casserole about 15 minutes before serving.

Lancashire hot-pot

cooking time: 2 hours

you will need:

12 oz. lean best neck of mutton or stewing steak	2 large onions salt and pepper hot water
1 lb. potatoes	1 oz. margarine

1 Cut the meat into neat pieces.
2 Peel and slice the potatoes and onions to about ¼ inch thick.
3 Fill a casserole with alternate layers of meat, potato and onion, ending with a layer of potato.
4 Sprinkle salt and pepper over each layer.
5 Half fill the casserole with hot water, put the margarine on top in small pieces.
6 Put on the lid and bake in the coolest part of the oven for 2 hours (350°F. – Gas Mark 3), or if baking a pudding in the oven at the same time, cook for 1½ hours (375°F. – Gas Mark 4).
7 Take the lid off for the last 20 minutes to brown the top.

Thrifty hot-pot

cooking time: 2½ hours

you will need:

2 lb. scrag end neck lamb	salt and pepper
1 oz. dripping	1 lb. potatoes
2 onions	½ pint stock
1 teaspoon mixed herbs	chopped parsley

1 Prepare, trim and cut the neck into pieces.
2 Fry the meat in a pan in the dripping.
3 Remove the meat and lightly fry the sliced onions.
4 Place a layer of meat, then a little of the onion and a sprinkling of the herbs and seasoning in a casserole dish.
5 Then cover with a layer of potatoes.
6 Repeat this process until all the ingredients have been used, finishing with a layer of potatoes.
7 Pour in the stock, cover with a lid and cook at 350°F. – Gas Mark 3 for about 2½ hours.
8 Half an hour before the end of the cooking time remove the lid and allow potatoes to brown.
9 Sprinkle chopped parsley on top and serve.

Lamb and rice casserole

cooking time: approximately 1 hour

you will need:

3 oz. butter	salt and pepper
2 good sized onions	cooked lamb
4 oz. rice	pinch nutmeg or
1½ pints water flavoured with yeast extract or stock	cinnamon ½ pint tomato sauce or purée

1 Heat 2 oz. butter in a pan.
2 Add the finely chopped onions and when tender add the rice.
3 Toss with the onion and butter, then pour in the stock or water.
4 Season well and cook for about 10 minutes until the rice has absorbed most of the liquid.
5 Add the lamb, cut into neat fingers, and the nutmeg and an extra 1 oz. butter.
6 Put into casserole.
7 Cover with lid and heat gently for about 40 minutes.
8 Serve with tomato sauce (see page 87) or purée of tomatoes.

Leg of mutton or cut of beef with broad beans

cooking time: 3 hours

you will need:

2 oz. butter	½ pint hot water
3 lb. piece leg mutton or cut beef (shoulder piece or vein piece)	1 lb. potatoes
	1 large can broad beans
1–2 meat extract cubes	

1 Melt butter in a casserole or large saucepan.
2 Add joint and brown the outside.
3 Remove joint.
4 Place 3 meat skewers in the bottom of the pan and place the joint on these.
5 Crumble beef cubes into the hot water.
6 Pour this gravy over the joint.
7 Cover the dish with a well-fitting lid and place in a very moderate oven (350°F. – Gas Mark 3). Cook for 2½–3 hours.
8 40 minutes before the end of the cooking time place potatoes around the joint. To obtain browned potatoes remove lid from casserole 15 minutes before the end of cooking time.
9 This pot-roast may be cooked on the top of cooker for same time.
10 Serve with broad beans.

Barbecued spare ribs

cooking time: 1¼ hours

you will need:

1 beef extract cube	1 level teaspoon salt
¼ pint hot water	2 teaspoons tomato paste
1 small onion	
2 tablespoons lemon juice	1 tablespoon Worcestershire sauce
1 level tablespoon brown sugar	4 thick chops or ribs pork
2 level tablespoons dry mustard	½ oz. butter or oil

1 Dissolve beef cube in the water.
2 Peel and chop the onion.
3 Add lemon juice.
4 Mix sugar, mustard and salt with the tomato paste, sauce and the liquids.
5 Place the chops in a wide shallow casserole and bake uncovered for about 30 minutes or until well browned in a moderately hot oven (400°F. – Gas Mark 5).
6 Pour off any fat.
7 Meanwhile, fry the onion in the butter or oil until brown.
8 Add remaining ingredients, pour over chops.
9 Cover and continue baking for about 45 minutes.

Tomato rolls

cooking time: 2¼ hours

you will need:

4 thin slices leg veal	1 finely chopped onion
1 oz. butter	little chopped parsley
seasoning	grated lemon rind

for sauce:

small onion	generous ½ pint water (or white stock)
tiny piece eating apple	
1 oz. butter or margarine	small can tomato purée
1 rounded teaspoon cornflour	seasoning

1 Spread each slice of veal with butter and sprinkle with seasoning, onion, parsley and lemon rind.
2 Roll firmly with the onion mixture inside – secure with skewers.

To make sauce:

3 Grate onion and apple and toss in butter for a few minutes, taking care they do not brown.
4 Blend cornflour and water, pour into saucepan.
5 Add tomato purée.
6 Bring to boil and cook until clear and smooth.
7 Season well.
8 Put the veal rolls into a casserole – cover with sauce and lid or foil.
9 Cook for approximately 2 hours in a slow oven (300°F. – Gas Mark 2).

Variations:

Veal rolls Provençal – fry 2 oz. chopped mushrooms and 2 chopped onions and a chopped clove of garlic in 2 oz. butter. Add tomato purée, water and cornflour as before.

Veal birds – spread slices of veal with your favourite stuffing, then roll. Cover with the tomato sauce or brown sauce. Cook as before. Serve with bacon rolls and diced root vegetables.

Veal and bacon rolls – spread stuffing on veal and roll, then roll rashers of bacon round each piece of veal. Tie and continue as for veal rolls. If bacon is reasonably fat, you can reduce the amount of dripping.

Italian pot pie

cooking time: 1 hour 10 minutes

you will need:

1 beef extract cube	1 oz. butter
¼ pint hot water	1 oz. flour
4 lamb's kidneys	parsley to garnish
4 large onions	

1 Dissolve beef extract cube in the hot water.

continued

2 Peel, wash and core kidneys.

3 Peel onions, and remove the centres until the cavity is large enough to hold a kidney.

4 Place onion centres in a casserole and put the stuffed onions on top.

5 Add gravy.

6 Bake in moderate oven (375°F. – Gas Mark 4) for 1 hour.

7 Strain off the liquid around the onions.

8 Melt the butter, stir in the flour and blend in the stock carefully.

9 Bring to the boil and cook until the sauce thickens.

10 Pour this round the cooked onions in the casserole and serve garnished with parsley.

Spanish rice with frankfurters

cooking time: 1 hour 25 minutes

you will need:

1 green pepper	1½ teaspoons salt
1 large onion, sliced	pinch ground cloves
3 tablespoons bacon	1 bay leaf
fat or oil	8 oz. uncooked rice
large can tomatoes	water
1 tablespoon sugar	8–10 split frankfurters

1 Chop pepper finely.

2 Fry onion in fat until tender.

3 Add the tomatoes, green pepper and seasonings.

4 Simmer for 10 minutes.

5 Stir in the rice, cover and simmer for about 45 minutes, adding water gradually to keep the mixture moist.

6 Arrange alternative layers of the rice mixture and frankfurter halves in a greased casserole and cover.

7 Bake in a moderate oven (375°F. – Gas Mark 4) for about 30 minutes.

Variations:

Family paella – an economical paella can be made by adding a few shelled prawns to the Spanish rice at stage 7, just before serving.

Party paella – use the recipe for Spanish rice, but only 3–4 frankfurters, then add 8–12 oz. diced raw chicken and fry with the onions at stage 2. Stir shelled prawns or other shellfish into the very hot rice at stage 7, just before serving.

Welcome home hot-pot

cooking time: 20 minutes, plus time of cooking stew

you will need:
your favourite stew recipe

for topping:

8 oz. plain flour	4 oz. lard and
¼ teaspoon salt	margarine mixed
2 level teaspoons	about 5 tablespoons
baking powder	milk
	egg and milk to glaze

1 Make your favourite stew the way you always do, but 20 minutes before it is cooked, remove casserole lid and put on this exciting scone mix topping.

2 Sieve plain flour, salt and baking powder.

3 Rub in fat until mixture resembles fine bread-crumbs.

4 Bind to a stiff dough with milk.

5 Knead lightly and roll out to ½ inch thickness.

6 Cut into rounds with a 2-inch cutter.

7 Place rounds on top of stew, brush with beaten egg or milk.

8 Return to moderately hot oven (400°F. – Gas Mark 5) for the last 20 minutes.

Gammon casserole

cooking time: 1 hour

you will need:

4 slices gammon	1 oz. seedless raisins
2 eating apples	(optional)
4 tomatoes	¼ pint cider
1 onion	pepper (no salt)

1 Remove skin from gammon and arrange in the casserole.

2 Core, but do not peel apples.

3 Cut each apple into half through the centre.

4 Arrange apples and whole tomatoes round gammon.

5 Cover with thinly sliced onion, raisins, and cider and a good pinch of pepper.

6 Put lid on casserole and cook for about 1 hour in centre of a moderate oven (375°F. – Gas Mark 4).

Bacon with raisin sauce

8–10 servings

cooking time: 2½ hours

you will need:

piece collar or hock
bacon approximately
2¼–3 lb.
about 12 tiny onions or
24 cocktail onions

2 sliced apples (sharp
apples in a dessert
variety are ideal)

for sauce:

1 good teaspoon
mustard powder
1 tablespoon brown
sugar

¼ pint cider
seasoning
4 oz. stoned raisins

1 Blend the mustard, sugar and cider together.
2 Add the seasoning and the raisins.
3 Put the piece of bacon into a casserole with the onions.
4 Cover with the sliced apples and pour the sauce round the side.
5 Put on lid or cover with aluminium foil.
6 Cook for approximately 2½ hours in a moderate oven (375°F. – Gas Mark 4).

Variation:

Bacon with sour sweet sauce – use the recipe for raisin sauce above, but add 2 tablespoons chopped vinegar pickles and a tablespoon honey as well as the sugar. In view of the extra sweetening in this sauce, you may need to reduce the heat after 1½ hours to make sure the mixture does not burn.

Bacon and beans casserole

cooking time: 2–2½ hours or longer on lower heat

you will need:

8 oz. dried butter
beans
1½ lb. forehock bacon
4 tomatoes
2 green peppers
(optional)
1 stick celery

1 onion
2 carrots
seasoning
½–1 pint stock, or
water with bouillon
cube

1 Soak butter beans overnight.
2 Strain off water.
3 Cut bacon into chunks.
4 Slice tomatoes and de-seeded peppers.
5 Chop the celery, onion and carrots.
6 Place all ingredients into a large casserole and season well.
7 Add the stock and cover tightly.
8 Cook for 2–2½ hours in a very moderate oven (325°F. – Gas Mark 3) or on lower marks for 4–5 hours.
9 Delicious served with jacket potatoes.

Barbecued bacon

5–6 servings

cooking time: 1¼ hours

you will need:

1¼–1½ lb. collar bacon
2 sliced dessert apples
2 very thinly sliced
onions
4 thickly sliced
tomatoes

¼ pint cider
seasoning
parsley to garnish
1 lb. mashed potatoes

1 Put the bacon into casserole with sliced apples (leaving skins on), onions and tomatoes.
2 Cover with cider, season well.
3 Bake in a covered dish for 1¼–1½ hours, in the centre of a very moderate oven (375°F. – Gas Mark 3–4).
4 Garnish with parsley. Serve with piped creamed potatoes and green vegetables.

Stews

As stated in the introduction to the meat chapter, many of the cheaper cuts of meat are **NOT** suitable for roasting, frying, etc. However, they are excellent for stews, as well as casserole dishes, and cooked in this way, are both delicious and economical. When making stews, do remember the following points:

1 In some recipes you will find the meat, vegetables etc., are first gently fried in fat. This gives added richness of flavour and should not be omitted.
2 NEVER hurry the cooking time, and make sure the lid of the pan fits tightly when stewing, as if too much moisture escapes from the pan the stew could burn, through lack of liquid.
If you are not entirely happy to leave the saucepan unattended, transfer the stew to the top of a double saucepan.

Beef Provençale

cooking time: 3¼ hours

you will need:

2 tablespoons olive oil
2 large onions
3 rashers bacon
1¼ lb. chuck steak, cut
   into neat fingers
seasoning
1 oz. flour
¼ pint cheap white
   wine*
  *This helps to tenderise the meat.

approximately ½ pint
   water
bunch mixed herbs
   (or good pinch
   dried herbs)
3 or 4 tomatoes
few olives to garnish

1 Heat the oil in the pan and fry the sliced onions and bacon.
2 Add the meat coated with well seasoned flour and toss in the oil for a few minutes.
3 Add all the other ingredients, except the olives.
4 Bring to the boil and cook for a few minutes until a fairly thick liquid.
5 Taste and re-season if desired.
6 Reduce the heat, put a lid on the pan and simmer gently for approximately 3 hours.
7 Remove bunch of herbs and pour on to a hot dish.
8 Garnish with olives and serve in a border of freshly cooked vegetables or cooked rice.

Variation:

Somerset beef – omit the white wine in the recipe above and use fairly dry cider instead. If you can obtain crab apples use about 12 of these or 2 cooking apples in place of olives. Either the whole crab apples or sliced cooking apples should be added at stage 6, after cooking the beef etc. for 1½ hours.

Brisket roundabout

cooking time: 2½–3 hours

you will need:

1 stock cube
¼ pint hot water
3 lb. boned brisket of
   beef
8 oz. sliced onions

½ oz. dripping or
   margarine
8 oz. skinned tomatoes
salt and pepper
1 large can butter
   beans

for stuffing:

2 oz. white bread-
   crumbs
2 teaspoons chopped
   parsley
½ teaspoon mixed
   herbs

salt and pepper
1 oz. chopped suet
grated rind ½ lemon
beaten egg to bind

to garnish:
chopped parsley

1 Dissolve beef cube in water.
2 Make stuffing by mixing all dry ingredients together and binding with a little beaten egg.
3 Spread stuffing on the meat, roll and tie firmly with fine string.
4 Fry onions in hot dripping until soft.
5 Add meat and tomatoes and pour over the liquid.
6 Season well, cover and cook slowly on the top of the stove or in a slow oven (300°F. – Gas Mark 2) for 2–3 hours.
7 15 minutes before the end of cooking add the canned butter beans.
8 Serve sprinkled with freshly chopped parsley.

Flemish beef stew

cooking time: 2¼ hours

you will need:

1 lb. diced flank of
   beef or stewing beef
2 sliced onions
2 oz. dripping or fat
2 sliced carrots
water

bay leaf
good pinch mixed
   herbs
1 thick slice bread
seasoning
mustard

1 Fry well seasoned meat and onions in the hot fat until golden brown.
2 Add carrots and 1¼ pints water.
3 Put in herbs and bay leaf. Season.
4 Simmer in a covered saucepan until meat is tender (this will take about 2 hours).
5 Remove crusts from slice of bread.
6 Spread both sides of bread with mustard and drop on top of the stew.
7 Cook for a further 5 minutes.
8 Then beat the bread into the stew.

Variation:

Hasty beef stew – use minced beef and grated onions and carrots in the recipe above. Fry the beef and onions as stage 1, add the carrots and 1 pint stock or use tomato juice then simmer, stirring from time to time, for about 45 minutes. Continue as stage 5 onwards.

Greek beef stew

cooking time: 2¼ hours

you will need:

1½ lb. lean stewing
   beef
3 tablespoons oil or fat
1 pint water
6 oz. can tomato paste
3 tablespoons cider
   vinegar
2¼ teaspoons salt

½ teaspoon black
   pepper
2 2-inch sticks
   cinnamon
1 onion, stuck with 8
   whole cloves
2 lb. small white
   onions

1 Cube the meat and brown on all sides in hot oil or fat.
2 Combine the water, tomato paste, vinegar, salt and pepper.
3 Heat to boiling point and pour over the meat.
4 Add the cinnamon and onion stuck with the cloves.
5 Cover and simmer until meat is tender.
6 Add the onions about 35 minutes before cooking time is up.

Beef in red wine

cooking time: 2¼ hours

you will need:

1½ lb. stewing beef, cut into cubes	pinch sugar
½ oz. seasoned flour	¼ pint red wine (scant measure)
1 oz. dripping	½ pint stock
2 rashers streaky bacon, cut in pieces	seasoning
12 small onions	*bouquet garni*
2 oz. mushrooms, peeled and sliced	

1 Roll cubes of beef in seasoned flour.
2 Melt dripping and add meat.
3 Brown well on all sides.
4 Remove meat and add bacon, onion, mushrooms, pinch sugar and brown gently again.
5 Take out mushrooms and onions.
6 Return meat.
7 Heat the wine and add it to meat.
8 Add stock to cover, seasoning and *bouquet garni*.
9 Cover and cook slowly for 1 hour.
10 Add onions and mushrooms and continue cooking for another hour.
11 Serve with chopped parsley and creamed potatoes.

Jugged beef

cooking time: 2½–3 hours

you will need:

2–3 meat cubes	2 onions
¾ pint hot water	2–4 cloves
1½ lb. shin beef	grated rind ½ lemon
2 oz. seasoned flour	*bouquet garni*
4 oz. chopped bacon	6 small mushrooms

1 Dissolve meat cubes in water.
2 Cut meat into 2-inch pieces and roll in the seasoned flour.
3 Chop bacon and fry in a saucepan.
4 Add the meat, browning lightly.
5 Add onions, cloves, lemon rind, *bouquet garni*, mushrooms and liquid.

6 Cover and cook slowly either on top of the stove or in a casserole in a slow oven (300°F. – Gas Mark 2) for 2½ to 3 hours.
7 Remove *bouquet garni*, onion and cloves before serving.

Goulash

cooking time: 2 hours

Use ingredients as for pressure cooked goulash on page 57, but cook in a saucepan for 1½ hours. Then add potatoes and continue cooking for further 30 minutes. You will need at least ½ pint stock.

Variation:

With veal – a mixture of beef and veal can be used.

Mexican mince

cooking time: 1¼ hours

you will need:

1 tablespoon olive oil	2 teaspoons Worcestershire sauce
2 chopped onions	4 oz. kidney beans or haricot beans, soaked overnight
2 crushed cloves garlic	
1 lb. minced beef	1 meat extract cube
¾ oz. flour	¼ pint hot water
6 tomatoes, skinned	salt

1 Heat olive oil in a saucepan and fry onions and garlic.
2 Add meat and brown lightly.
3 Sprinkle on the flour and then add tomatoes cut into quarters, sauce, beans, meat cube dissolved in water and salt to taste.
4 Cover and cook slowly either on top of the stove or in a casserole in a slow oven (300°F. – Gas Mark 2) for 1 hour.

Savoury mince with chestnuts

cooking time: 1¼ hours

you will need:

8 oz. cooked meat	1 oz. fat for sauce
1 lb. chestnuts	1 oz. flour
1 onion	salt and pepper
4 cloves	fat or butter
stock	

1 Mince the meat.
2 Cut a small piece of skin off each chestnut, place in cold water and bring to the boil. *continued*

41

3 Skin them while warm and put in a saucepan with the onion, cloves and stock to cover.

4 Simmer gently for 1 hour, and strain, keeping the liquid. If necessary add water to make ½ pint.

5 Melt the fat, fry the flour until brown, add the liquid, and boil.

6 Reheat the minced meat in the sauce, season, and dish up in a border of chestnuts, tossed in a little fat or butter.

Oxtail ragoût

cooking time: 4 hours

you will need:

1 medium-sized oxtail	4 small carrots, thickly sliced
cornflour or flour for coating	1 small turnip, in large dice
salt and pepper	
little fat	2 sticks celery, in large dice
4 oz. bacon – diced	
1 medium onion	14 oz. can tomatoes
4 cloves	¾ pint water
bouquet garni	1 beef extract cube
1 clove garlic, crushed	1–2 leeks, sliced

1 Remove any excess fat from oxtail and cut into serving pieces.

2 Blanch in boiling water, drain and dry.

3 Coat the pieces in cornflour or flour to which salt and pepper have been added.

4 Heat the fat in a pan and sauté the pieces of oxtail and bacon till golden.

5 Pour off any excess fat in the pan.

6 Add the onion stuck with cloves, *bouquet garni*, garlic and all vegetables except the leeks.

7 Add the tomatoes, water and crumbled beef cube.

8 Simmer for 3–4 hours.

9 30 minutes before end of cooking time, add the sliced leeks.

Panned pork chops

cooking time: 1¼ hours

you will need:

4 pork chops	1 level tablespoon brown sugar
2 oz. butter	
1 pint sieved tomato	1 teaspoon Worcestershire sauce
about ¼ pint of water	seasoning

1 Trim the chops and brown on both sides in butter with all other ingredients.

2 Cover the pan and simmer gently for 1 hour or until the meat is tender.

3 Serve with creamed potatoes and Brussels sprouts.

Winter beef stew

cooking time: 1½–2 hours

you will need:

1 skirt of beef	1 oz. grated cheese
8 oz. minced pork or sausage meat	salt and pepper
	1 potato
1 egg	1 onion
1 teaspoon chopped parsley	1 beef extract cube

1 Slit the beef down the middle, taking care that only one side is opened. (The butcher will do this for you.)

2 In a bowl, mix the pork, egg, parsley and cheese.

3 Add salt and pepper.

4 Mix all ingredients thoroughly.

5 Fill up the skirt with this mixture.

6 Using white cotton, sew up the slit in the skirt.

7 Put the skirt with a sliced potato, a sliced onion and a crumbled beef extract cube in a saucepan.

8 Just cover with water.

9 Bring the water to the boil.

10 Lower the heat and simmer for 1½ hours or until the meat is tender.

11 When ready, take the skirt out of the soup and cut into slices.

12 To serve: First serve the soup with fried or toasted bread cut into cubes. Serve the sliced skirt with sauté potatoes and fried onions.

Oxtail

cooking time: 2½ hours

Recipe as for pressure cooked oxtail, see page 57, but simmer in saucepan in 1½ pints water for 2½ hours.

Some people find this dish over 'fatty' in which case cook previous day and allow to cool. Then remove the fat from the top of the dish.

Brawn

cooking time: 3 hours

you will need:

1 pig's head or 6 pig's trotters	2 bay leaves
	seasoning
8 oz. stewing beef (not essential)	pinch mixed herbs
	small bunch parsley

1 After washing pig's head or trotters well, put into a large saucepan and cover with water.

2 Simmer gently for 1 hour.

3 Remove from the stock which should be saved.

4 Cut all meat from head or trotters, removing any gristle and bones.

5 Cut meat and stewing beef into neat small dice.

6 Return the meat to the stock, adding bay leaves, seasoning, pinch herbs and the bunch of parsley.

7 Simmer gently for 1½–2 hours until the meat feels quite tender.

8 Take out the parsley and pour into a rinsed mould or large basin. Allow to set.

Variation:

Tongue brawn – omit the stewing beef in the recipe above and simmer 1 or 2 small lamb's tongues with the pig's head or trotters. Cut these in neat pieces, skinning and removing bones, and mix with the meat from the head or trotters at stage 6. If preferred, buy about 6–8 oz. cooked tongue (in one piece), dice and add to the rest of the ingredients at stage 8.

Haricot mutton

cooking time: 2½ hours

you will need:

4 oz. haricot beans	1 oz. flour
1 oz. lard or dripping	1 pint water or stock
1 large onion	salt and pepper
1 sweet red pepper	few potatoes
1 lb. stewing mutton	parsley to garnish

1 Soak haricot beans overnight in cold water, leaving plenty of room in the container for the beans to swell.

2 Heat the lard in the saucepan and fry the sliced onion, chopped pepper and meat, cut into neat pieces, for a few minutes.

3 Stir in the flour and cook this gently for about 5 minutes, stirring all the time.

4 Gradually add the cold stock or water.

5 Bring to the boil, stirring well until the stock has boiled and thickened slightly.

6 Add haricot beans, well drained, and seasoning.

7 Simmer gently for nearly 2 hours.

8 Slice the potatoes on top of the mutton stew adding a good pinch of salt and pepper.

9 Cook for a further 25 minutes until the potatoes are tender.

10 To dish up, lift the sliced potatoes carefully from the stew, put these on a hot dish, pour the haricot mutton on top.

11 Garnish with sprigs of parsley.

Boiled breast of lamb

cooking time: 1¼–1½ hours

you will need:

breast lamb	1 pint hot water
stuffing (see page 88)	1 onion
1–2 meat extract cubes	

1 Ask the butcher to leave breast in one piece. Remove small bones and any surplus fat.

2 Make stuffing – spread on lamb.

3 Roll it up and tie firmly with string.

4 Crumble and dissolve meat cubes in 1 pint hot water.

5 Place meat and a chopped onion in a saucepan and pour over liquid.

6 Cover the pan and boil until the meat is tender – about 1¼–1½ hours.

7 Remove meat.

8 Serve hot with mixed vegetables and the gravy, or cold with salad.

Lamb soubise

cooking time: 1¾ hours

you will need:

piece best end neck of lamb	1–2 meat extract cubes
1 oz. butter	1 pint hot water
1½ lb. onions	salt and pepper
2 carrots	4 oz. rice
	parsley, to garnish

1 Ask your butcher to bone and roll the meat.

2 Melt butter in a thick saucepan.

3 Add the meat and brown the outside for a few minutes.

4 Peel and chop 1 onion and the carrots.

5 Crumble and dissolve beef cubes in 1 pint hot water.

6 Add the vegetables and bones and gravy to the meat and simmer slowly for 1¼ hours. Season.

7 Remove the meat and strain the stock.

8 Wash the saucepan, then return the meat and stock to it.

9 Put in rice and remaining chopped onions and cook until the rice is soft, about 15 minutes.

10 Serve the meat cut into rounds.

11 Sieve the rice and onions, which will have absorbed most of the stock in the saucepan.

12 Serve separately in a sauceboat.

13 Sprinkle chopped parsley on the soubise sauce.

Fricassée of lamb or mutton

cooking time: 2 hours

you will need:

8 pieces middle or scrag end lamb or mutton	½ pint milk
	few cooked peas
4 carrots	4 oz. Patna rice
2 onions	2 large slices bread
seasoning	little fat for frying
2 oz. butter	bread
2 oz. flour	chopped parsley
	paprika pepper

1 Simmer lamb with halved carrots and chopped

onions until just tender – about 1½ hours.
2 Season well.
3 Make a thick sauce of the butter, flour and milk.
4 Add ½ pint of the meat stock and stir until quite smooth.
5 Add the meat, carrots and peas to this.
6 Heat gently.
7 Serve in a border of boiled rice and garnish with triangles of fried bread, chopped parsley and paprika pepper.

Variation:

Fricassée of chicken – use a small jointed chicken instead of lamb or mutton. Shorten cooking time at stage 1 to 1 hour. Cook with the same vegetables as for lamb, but flavour with grated lemon rind at stage 4. This is delicious garnished with hot cooked prunes instead of fried bread.

Stewed breast of lamb

cooking time: 1¼ hours

you will need:

1 onion	1 oz. dripping or lard
1 carrot	1½ pints stock or water
1 stick celery	1 medium potato
1 breast of lamb, boned	2 tablespoons pearl
2 tablespoons flour	barley
salt and pepper	

1 Chop onion and slice other vegetables.
2 Wipe the meat with a damp cloth.
3 Trim away any excess fat and cut the meat into pieces about 2 inches square.
4 Toss the meat in seasoned flour.
5 Melt the fat and lightly fry the onion, carrot and celery.
6 Add meat and continue frying for a few minutes.
7 Add stock, potato and seasoning.
8 Bring to the boil and sprinkle in the pearl barley.
9 Reduce the heat and simmer for about 1 hour.
10 Reseason if necessary.

Pork sausage casserole

cooking time: 40 minutes

you will need:

2 large onions	½ pint water or stock
2 oz. lard	seasoning
2 large carrots, grated	1 lb. pork sausages
3 large tomatoes	little chopped parsley
1 oz. flour	bacon (optional)

1 Fry the very thinly sliced onions in the hot lard.
2 Add the grated carrots and sliced skinned tomatoes.

3 When soft, work in the flour.
4 Cook for a minute or so, then add the stock gradually.
5 Bring to the boil and cook until smooth and thickened.
6 Season well.
7 Add sausages and simmer gently for about 25 minutes.
8 Serve sprinkled with the parsley and top with bacon rolls if wished.

Variations:

Beef sausage casserole – follow recipe as above but use beef sausages instead of pork and beer instead of water or stock.
Sausage and leek casserole – use 1 lb. leeks in place of onion and carrots. Wash and slice the leeks, fry in the hot lard as stage 1 above, then add the sliced skinned tomatoes and continue as the recipe for the pork sausage casserole.

Osso bucco

cooking time: 1½ hours

you will need:

2 veal hocks	2 meat extract cubes
1 oz. olive oil	1 pint water
1 carrot	salt and pepper
2 onions	grated rind ½ lemon
1 small can tomatoes	parsley
bouquet garni	Parmesan cheese

1 Cut veal into 3-inch pieces.
2 Heat the olive oil and fry the meat, carrot and onions until browned.
3 Add the tomatoes, *bouquet garni* and the 2 meat cubes, crumbled and dissolved in hot water.
4 Season with salt and pepper.
5 Cover and cook until tender – about 1½ hours.
6 Remove the *bouquet garni* and serve sprinkled with lemon rind and parsley.
7 Serve with boiled rice and grated Parmesan cheese sprinkled on top.

Fricassée of veal

cooking time: 1¾ hours

you will need:

1¼ lb. stewing veal	1–2 onions
1 pint white stock or	lemon
water with chicken	2 oz. butter
bouillon cube	2 oz. flour
seasoning	½ pint milk

1 Cut the veal into neat fingers.
2 Put in a pan with water and chicken bouillon cube, or stock, seasoning, onion and thinly-pared lemon rind.

3 Simmer steadily for 1¼ hours.

4 Make a thick sauce of the butter, flour and milk.

5 Add ½ pint veal liquid and when the sauce is quite smooth add the veal.

6 Heat gently, whisk in lemon juice before serving.

7 Serve with creamed potatoes or boiled rice.

Veal Marengo

cooking time: 1¼ hours

you will need:

1 lb. neck veal	½ pint white stock or
little flour	water
seasoning	8 oz. skinned tomatoes
3 oz. butter or 3	2 oz. mushrooms
tablespoons oil	4 slices bread
2 finely chopped	fat for frying
onions or shallots	parsley
	lemon

1 Cut the meat into neat pieces.

2 Coat with a thin layer of seasoned flour and fry until pale golden brown in the hot butter or oil.

3 Add finely diced onions and fry until transparent.

4 Add stock, chopped tomatoes and mushrooms.

5 Season well.

6 Simmer gently for approximately 1 hour.

7 Serve garnished with croûtons of fried bread, parsley and lemon.

Fried veal with rice

cooking time: 1 hour

you will need:

4 neck of veal cutlets	1 stick celery
seasoned flour	1 tomato
1 small onion	3 oz. fat or oil
1 small green sweet	¼ pint stock
pepper	8 oz. rice

1 Toss the cutlets in seasoned flour.

2 Peel and chop the onion and chop other vegetables.

3 Melt 2 oz. fat and fry the veal until brown on both sides.

4 Add the stock, or water and meat cube.

5 Simmer the meat until it is tender (45 minutes).

6 Boil the rice.

7 Melt 1 oz. fat and fry the onion, green pepper and celery.

8 Stir in the cooked rice and add the tomato.

9 Serve the cutlets on top of the rice mixture and pour over the juices from the frying pan.

Variation:

Parmesan veal and rice – continue as the recipe above; arrange the cutlets on the bed of rice,

top with a thick layer of grated Parmesan (or other cooking cheese). Heat for a few minutes under the grill, then add the juices from the frying pan and serve.

Liver pilaf

cooking time: 25 minutes

you will need:

½ aubergine	1 oz. seasoned flour
1 large tomato	4 oz. mushrooms
6 oz. Patna rice	¼ pint boiling salted
1 meat cube	water
1 lb. calves' liver	1 oz. butter

1 Slice aubergine and tomato.

2 Put rice, tomato, aubergine and meat cube into a saucepan and cover with boiling water.

3 Cover and cook gently on the top of the stove for 20–25 minutes or until the rice has absorbed all the water.

4 Meanwhile, cut liver into small pieces and toss in seasoned flour.

5 Peel and slice mushrooms.

6 Melt the butter and fry the liver for a few minutes.

7 Add mushrooms and liquid.

8 Cover and simmer gently for 15–20 minutes.

9 Make a ring of rice and vegetables on a hot serving dish and pour the liver and mushrooms in the centre.

Variation:

Lamb pilaf – dice about 1 lb. lean lamb (cut from the leg) and use in place of the liver. The cooking time at stage 8 should be extended to 35 minutes, use a little extra liquid so meat does not dry.

Bacon stew with kidney dumplings

cooking time: 1¼ hours

you will need:

2–3 meaty bacon	1 parsnip
bones	2 small onions

for dumplings:

4 oz. sheeps' kidney	salt and pepper
1 oz. butter	1½ oz. shredded suet
4 oz. self-raising flour	cold water to mix

1 Place the bacon bones in a pan with cold water, bring to the boil, then discard water.

2 Add fresh water to cover and add the chopped parsnip and onions.

3 Simmer gently for 1½ hours.

4 Cook the kidneys in butter, chop finely or put through mincer. *continued*

5 Mix together the flour, seasoning and suet, stir in the kidney and mix to a fairly soft dough with water.

6 Form into small balls, add these to the stew and continue cooking for 10–20 minutes.

Variation:

Bacon and herb dumplings – use the recipe above, but omit the kidney. Instead dice 2–3 rashers of bacon, fry until crisp then add to the flour etc. at stage 5, together with a teaspoon of freshly chopped herbs.

Ham in Cumberland sauce

cooking time: 15 minutes

you will need:
8 thin or 4 thicker
  slices cooked ham

for sauce:

¼ pint water	2 tablespoons water
grated rind and juice	(or port wine for
1 lemon	special occasions)
grated rind and juice	3 tablespoons red-
2 oranges	currant or apple jelly
1 teaspoon cornflour	
or arrowroot	

1 Put the water and grated fruit rinds into a saucepan and simmer for about 5 minutes.

2 Strain if wished, then return the liquid to pan, but if you grate the rinds finely they are very soft and look attractive in the sauce.

3 Add the fruit juice and the cornflour or arrow-root blended with the 2 tablespoons water or wine.

4 Bring to the boil and add jelly.

5 Cook until clear.

6 Put in ham and heat gently for a few minutes only so that the meat remains a pleasant pink colour.

7 Serve at once with garden peas and cooked corn on the cob.

Variation:

With mustard – the sauce can be varied in flavour by adding made mustard to taste, or pepper or a little salt.

Braised Dishes

Braising meat

The term 'braising' means a combination of roasting and stewing. In most of the following recipes, you will find that the meat is first cooked in fat, then simmered in a thick rich sauce, thus giving a rather more succulent result than in an ordinary stew or casserole dish.

Beef olives

cooking time: 2 hours

you will need:

1 lb. stewing meat or	seasoning
top side beef	1 bay leaf
1 onion	¾ pint stock or water
1 carrot	with meat cube
2 oz. fat	1 oz. flour

for veal forcemeat:

2 oz. fresh	½ level teaspoon
breadcrumbs	grated lemon rind
1–2 oz. suet	pinch salt
1 tablespoon chopped	salt and pepper
parsley	1 egg
1 level teaspoon dried	milk to mix
thyme or savory	

1 Ask your butcher to thinly slice top rump or chuck steak into pieces about 4 × 3 inches.

2 Prepare the forcemeat by combining all in-gredients.

3 Spread some on each piece of flattened, beaten meat, roll up and secure with thick white cotton or very fine string.

4 Peel and slice the onion and carrot.

5 Heat the fat and fry the onion and beef olives in it; add the carrot and seasoning, bay leaf and stock.

6 Stir in flour and cook until thickened.

7 Cover and simmer until tender, or transfer to a covered casserole.

8 Remove string before serving.

Variation:

Sausage stuffed olives – instead of the stuffing above blend 8 oz. pork or beef sausagemeat with 2 teaspoons chopped parsley, ½ teaspoon chopped sage and bind with an egg.

Apple spare rib

cooking time: 10–15 minutes

you will need:

4 spare rib pork chops	1 oz. lard
1 egg	¼ pint stock, or water
sage and onion	and meat cube
stuffing*	2 Bramley apples
(see page 88)	

*or packet stuffing.

1 Dip the chops in the beaten egg, then the sage and onion stuffing.
2 Melt the lard, fry the chops on both sides until golden brown.
3 Add the meat cube and water, or stock, and leave on a low heat for 10–15 minutes until the chops are cooked through.
4 Remove chops and place on one side to keep warm.
5 Add the peeled, cored and chopped apples to the frying pan and cook until they are reduced to pulp.
6 Place a spoonful of the apple mixture on each chop and pour extra juice around the chops.

Braised hand of pork

cooking time: 3 hours

you will need:

1 lb. onions	3–3½ lb. hand of pork
1 lb. carrots	salt and pepper
8 oz. tomatoes	2 meat cubes
1 oz. dripping	½ pint hot water

1 Peel the onions and carrots and cut them into pieces with the tomatoes.
2 Melt the dripping in a saucepan and brown the meat.
3 Remove from the pan and put in the vegetables.
4 Fry for a few minutes.
5 Turn the vegetables into a casserole and place the meat on top.
6 Season well.
7 Crumble and dissolve the meat cubes in the hot water and pour this gravy over the joint.
8 Cover the casserole.
9 Cook in moderate oven (375°F. – Gas Mark 4) for 2½–3 hours.
10 Serve the sliced meat surrounded by vegetables, and hand gravy separately. This may be thickened by blending in 1 oz. flour and bringing to the boil.

Barbecued lamb

cooking time: 2 hours

you will need:

2 pieces middle neck lamb	1 teaspoon salt
2 tablespoons oil or 2 oz. fat	pinch each pepper, dry mustard, paprika
¾ pint water	½ teaspoon each celery seed, basil, oregano
3 tablespoons vinegar	
½ pint canned orange juice	5 whole cloves
2 teaspoons Worcestershire sauce	2 teaspoons sugar

1 Brown pieces of lamb in hot corn oil, or fat, in pan.
2 Add water and vinegar; simmer for 1 hour.
3 Remove lid and boil rapidly until liquid is reduced to about ½ pint.
4 Cook and skim.
5 Meanwhile combine the orange juice, Worcestershire sauce, seasonings and sugar in small saucepan.
6 Simmer for 10 minutes.
7 Add to the lamb, stirring carefully to blend with the broth.
8 Cover and simmer a further 45 minutes, or until lamb is tender.
9 Serve with boiled rice.

Braised best end of neck

cooking time: 2 hours

you will need:

1 best end of neck lamb or mutton	1 stick celery
2 onions	2 oz. dripping or lard
2 carrots	stock
1 turnip	salt and pepper

1 Remove the chine bone and flap from the joint and wipe the meat with a damp cloth.
2 Prepare and roughly dice the vegetables.
3 Melt the dripping in a pan and brown the meat quickly.
4 Remove the meat and add the vegetables.
5 Brown them gently, then place the joint on top.
6 Add sufficient stock to just cover the vegetables.
7 Season, cover the pan and cook gently for about 1½ hours.
8 Place the pan uncovered in a moderately hot oven (400°F. – Gas Mark 5) for about 30 minutes to brown and crisp the fat.
9 Serve on a dish with additional assorted root vegetables cut into strips, and boiled.

Note:

The joint may also be cooked with the vegetables in a very moderate oven (350°F. – Gas Mark 4) for the whole of the cooking time, about 1¾ hours.

Devilled pork and beans

cooking time: 2 hours

you will need:

4 oz. haricot beans*	good pinch curry
approximately 1¼ lb.	powder
belly of pork	½–1 tablespoon Wor-
1 oz. margarine	cestershire sauce
2 good sized onions	1 tablespoon tomato
1 oz. flour	ketchup
½ pint stock or water	2 teaspoons mustard
	seasoning

*or use canned haricot beans in tomato sauce and omit tomato ketchup.

1 Soak beans overnight (unless using canned haricot beans).
2 Simmer until nearly tender.
3 Dice pork and fry gently in the margarine.
4 Add chopped onions and cook gently in the hot margarine and pork fat.
5 Stir in flour and cook again for several minutes.
6 Add stock, sauces, beans, flavourings and seasonings.
7 Bring to boil and when thickened transfer to casserole.
8 Cover well and cook gently for 1½–2 hours.

Braised breast of mutton

cooking time: 2–2¼ hours

you will need:

breast mutton	approximately 1 lb.
flour	diced mixed
seasoning	vegetables
2 onions	2–3 large skinned
	tomatoes

1 Coat breast of mutton – which need not be boned – with a good layer of seasoned flour.
2 Fry steadily in a large pan until golden brown on both sides.
3 If pan is not large enough, cut into pieces, also add a little fat.*
4 Lift out of pan into casserole.
5 Toss sliced onions in fat in the pan.

6 Spread over meat in casserole.
7 Add all vegetables, chopping tomatoes coarsely.
8 Cover with about ½ pint boiling water and put on lid.
9 Cook steadily for about 1½–2 hours in a very moderate oven (325°F.–350°F. – Gas Mark 2–3).

*Most breasts of mutton are sufficiently fat, but you need enough fat coming from the meat to brown it well and fry the onions.

Variation:

Braised pork chops – use 4 good sized pork chops instead of the breast of mutton, continue as stages 1–2. Add a little sage to the onions at stage 6 and 1 large thinly sliced apple or about 8 soaked, but not cooked, prunes at stage 8.

Braised heart

cooking time: 2 hours

Follow recipe for pressure cooked heart on page 58, allowing 1 pint stock, and instead of pressure cooking, put into a casserole and cover.

Allow 2 hours in a very moderate oven (350°F. – Gas Mark 3) or simmer for about 1¾ hours in a covered saucepan.

Sausage jambalaya

cooking time: 1 hour 20 minutes

you will need:

1 lb. sausages	1 red pepper
2 onions, chopped	salt and pepper to
finely	taste
1 clove garlic	few oysters (optional)
1 medium can	6–8 oz. rice
tomatoes or 8 oz.	8 oz. shrimps or
skinned tomatoes	prawns

1 Fry the sausages steadily until brown.
2 Add onions and chopped garlic and cook in fat until clear.
3 Add tomatoes and chopped pepper and simmer slowly for 1 hour, adding water as needed. Season.
4 Add oysters and 1½ pints water and raw rice.
5 Bring to boil.
6 Cover tightly and simmer for 20 minutes.
7 Add shrimps or prawns at the last 10 minutes.
8 Serve immediately.

Braised veal and ham

cooking time: 2 hours

you will need:

1 onion	seasoning
3 tomatoes	¾ pint stock (or water
2 oz. lard	with yeast extract)
12 oz. stewing veal	6 oz. boiled bacon or
1 oz. flour	ham

1 Fry the sliced onion and skinned sliced tomatoes in the hot lard until tender, but not browned.

2 Add the veal rolled in the seasoned flour and cut into neat fingers.
3 Gradually cook until golden coloured.
4 Stir in the stock.
5 Bring to the boil and cook until thickened and smooth.
6 Season well.
7 Simmer gently for 1 hour.
8 Add fingers of the boiled bacon or ham and cook for a further 45 minutes.
9 Serve with creamed potatoes.

Poultry and Game Dishes

Choosing and cooking poultry

Due to improved methods of breeding, it is possible to purchase a much cheaper and wider range of poultry today. A great variety of chickens of all possible types are available – small birds for frying and grilling, large ones for roasting, and older fowls for steaming, boiling and so on.

A great deal of this poultry is frozen, and it is most important to remember that it MUST be defrosted before cooking. This should be done slowly at room temperature.

Tables for cooking poultry

Chicken

Method	Cooking time
Roasting: All chickens, whether small or large, need covering with fat over the breast. Use cheap fat bacon, cooking fat, or butter. Cover breast of bird with buttered paper, if you wish it to be golden brown.	15 minutes per lb. and 15 minutes over (weight to include stuffing). Start in hot oven then reduce to moderate.
Boiling: For older birds, allow 2½–3 hours depending on size. The water must simmer very gently.	For older birds, allow 2½–3 hours, depending on size.
Frying and Grilling	Approximately 20 minutes cooking time.

Turkey

Method	Cooking time
Roasting: As for chicken, but if not stuffing turkey, put a piece of butter inside body cavity to keep flesh moist.	As for chicken, but use moderate oven. Large birds need only 12 minutes per lb. for any weight above 12 lb.

Duck and duckling

Method	Cooking time
Roasting: A little fat is sometimes used in early stages of roasting a young duckling, but is not really necessary. To reduce fat, prick skin gently with a fine skewer, after the duck has been roasting about 30 minutes. If wished, brush skin with melted honey about 10 minutes before serving, to encourage a golden brown crisp skin.	As for chicken.

Goose

Method	Cooking time
Roasting: Prick two or three times during cooking. If a great deal of fat is flowing, pour it off during the cooking process. This helps to crisp outside of bird, and protect oven.	As for chicken.

Game

Method

Roasting: Cover with plenty of fat, as most game tends to be rather dry.

Cooking time

Roast in moderately hot oven. **Pheasant,** and **guinea fowl** are cooked as for chicken. **Rabbit** requires 20 minutes per lb. and 20 minutes over. **Small birds,** such as partridge require a total cooking time of about 30 minutes.

Stuffed roast chicken

cooking time: depending on weight of chicken

you will need:

1 chicken, 5–6 lb. in weight

butter or bacon fat

for stuffing:

1 oz. blanched almonds
1 medium raw onion
4 oz. mushrooms
uncooked liver from chicken

8 oz. white bread-crumbs
1 egg
seasoning

1 Toast the almonds until golden brown. Chop coarsely.
2 Peel and chop the onion and mushrooms finely. Chop the liver.
3 Put breadcrumbs into a basin. Pour over enough warm water to cover. Leave for 30 minutes. Drain off excess water.
4 Mix all the other ingredients with the bread. Add the beaten egg. Season well.
5 Put into chicken and roast for 15 minutes per lb. and 15 minutes over in a hot oven *or*
6 Allow 25 minutes per lb. at 350°F. – Gas Mark 3.

Note:

Cover the breast of the chicken well with butter or bacon fat before roasting and if using a covered roaster or foil, remove for the last 15 or 20 minutes to brown.

Variations in stuffing:

Giblet stuffing – add the chopped **cooked** giblets to the stuffing mixture above.

Sausage, raisin and walnut stuffing – add 2–3 oz. seedless raisins and 3–4 oz. chopped walnuts to 12 oz. pork sausagemeat.

Roast rabbit

cooking time: 1½ hours

you will need:

1 rabbit
either sage and onion or veal stuffing (see page 88) or 8 oz. sausage meat

fat
about 4–5 rashers streaky bacon

1 Wash rabbit as described in devilled rabbit (see page 56) and dry well.
2 Stuff the body of the rabbit (the head can be left on, although most people today like to remove this before cooking).
3 Heat knob of fat in roasting tin and spoon the hot fat over the rabbit.
4 Cover top with the bacon and put on lid or cover with foil over the tin.
5 Cook for about 1½ hours in the centre of a moderately hot oven (400°F. – Gas Mark 5), turning the heat down for the last 15 minutes if necessary.
6 Serve with roast potatoes and a green vegetable.
7 The liver, etc., of the rabbit can be simmered to give stock for gravy.

Note:

If you are not using sage and onion stuffing, an onion sauce (see page 87) is excellent with roast rabbit.

Ducks with apricot sauce

cooking time: depending on size of duck

you will need:

2 small ducklings or 1 larger duck

very little honey

for sauce:

1 medium sized can apricot halves
squeeze lemon juice
3 level teaspoons arrowroot or cornflour

2–3 tablespoons apricot brandy

to garnish:
watercress

1 Roast the ducks for approximately 1¼–1½ hours, depending on size, in a hot oven.
2 After they have been cooking for just about 45 minutes take out of the oven.
3 With a fine skewer break the skin only to enable any surplus fat to run out. BE VERY CARE-FUL NOT TO INSERT THE SKEWER TOO DEEPLY FOR IF YOU DO YOU WILL FIND THE FAT RUNS INTO THE DUCK RATHER THAN OUT.

4 Brush over the birds with a little warm honey to make sure you have a really crisp brown skin.

5 Put back again into hot oven and continue cooking.

6 A little time before the ducks are ready to dish up, make the sauce. Strain the liquid from the can of apricots.

7 Add the juice of the lemon and, if necessary, enough water to give just under $\frac{1}{2}$ pint liquid.

8 Blend with the arrowroot.

9 Put into the saucepan and cook until smooth, thickened and clear.

10 Taste and if necessary add a small amount of sugar or honey for the sauce should be slightly sweet but not sticky.

11 To give a shine to the sauce, you can either add a spoonful of strained fat from the ducks, or a small knob of butter.

12 Dish up the ducks.

13 Put the apricot halves into the sauce and heat for just a few moments.

14 Stir in the apricot brandy and heat but do not boil.

15 Pour over the ducks. Garnish with watercress.

Variation:
Ducks with cherry sauce – use canned black or Morello cherries in place of apricots and flavour with cherry brandy at stage 14.

Rôtisserie cooked chicken

Many modern cookers have a rôtisserie spit, either in the oven, or under the grill. The chicken is put on the rod, brushed with melted butter or fat, and cooked on the turning spit. Timing as for roasting (see tables, page 49).

Frying chicken

The small spring chickens, or broiler chickens as they are often called, can be grilled or fried.

To fry in shallow fat:
1 Coat the jointed chicken (to joint chicken, see right), with seasoned flour or with a little flour then egg and breadcrumbs.

2 Heat the fat in a pan – allowing about $\frac{1}{2}$ inch fat or oil.

3 Fry the joints steadily until golden brown on the under side, then turn other side.

4 Lower the heat to make sure the flesh is cooked through to the bone.

5 Serve with fried mushrooms, tomatoes, and crisp green salad.

To fry in deep fat:
1 If wished, coat the jointed chicken with egg and crumbs or with batter.

2 Make sure fat is hot to ensure quick browning and a crisp outside.

3 Brown chicken on both sides.

4 Lower the heat and cook steadily until crisp and golden and cooked through to the middle. With deep fat the chicken will be cooked within 15 minutes.

5 Drain well on absorbent paper, and serve with salad.

To joint a chicken for frying or grilling

1 Use a sharp, not too long knife or large kitchen scissors. First cut away the thighs and drum sticks, you will find this quite easy if you 'locate' the bone that joins the thigh to the body of the bird.

2 Cut down the centre – very slightly to one side of the breast bone – making two joints of breast and wings.

3 Cut away the rest of the body, there is so little meat on this that it is not worth grilling or frying, but can be used for stock.

4 If wished the thighs and drum sticks can be divided and the wings could be cut away from the breast to give a total of 8 pieces, but most people prefer 4 good sized joints.

5 If the birds are very small just divide into halves, so each half consists of breast, wing, one thigh and drum stick – flatten slightly for easy cooking.

Chicken Cordon Bleu

cooking time: 15–20 minutes

you will need:

2 small frying chickens*	little seasoned flour
4 slices ham	egg and breadcrumbs for coating
4 slices Gruyère or Cheddar cheese	fat for frying

*make sure they have nice meaty breasts

1 Use a sharp knife and cut away the breasts from the 2 chickens.

2 Slit them in half lengthways and sandwich together with ham and cheese.

3 Dip first in a little seasoned flour and then in egg and breadcrumbs.

4 Fry until crisp and golden brown in hot fat, then lower the heat and cook steadily for about 15–20 minutes.

Fried chicken and almonds

cooking time: 20 minutes

you will need:

1 jointed frying chicken	4 tablespoons soft breadcrumbs or crushed cornflakes
little flour	3 oz. butter or oil
seasoning	1–2 oz. blanched shredded almonds
egg	

1 Coat the chicken in seasoned flour, then beaten egg and crumbs.
2 Fry the chicken steadily in the hot butter or oil until golden brown.
3 Lower the heat and continue cooking for approximately 15 minutes until quite tender. Turn the chicken to brown evenly.
4 Transfer to hot serving dish.
5 Add extra knob of butter to pan and when hot toss the almonds in this.
6 Pour over the chicken and serve with vegetables or a salad.

Variation:

With lemon and parsley – almonds can be omitted and a little grated lemon rind and chopped parsley tossed in butter can be used instead.

Spiced chicken

cooking time: 40–45 minutes

you will need:

3 lb. young chicken	1-inch stick cinnamon
3 oz. butter	1–2 cloves garlic
1–2 teaspoons powdered turmeric	3 large onions
1 teaspoon ground ginger	salt
6 cloves	rice or noodles, to serve

1 Cut the uncooked chicken in about 12 joints, i.e. 4 from breast, 4 from wings, 4 from legs.
2 Skin the chicken and dry it thoroughly after washing.
3 Heat the butter and add the turmeric to it.
4 Put in the chicken pieces.
5 Raise the heat and fry the chicken for 7–8 minutes.
6 Add the ginger, cloves and splintered cinnamon.
7 Stir, then add chopped garlic and onions.
8 Sprinkle with salt and put on the lid of the pan.
9 Raise the heat to high for 10 seconds, then lower to medium.
10 Shake the pan, return to the heat and cook, without uncovering it, but shaking the pan from time to time, for about 25 minutes – longer if the broiler is older or seems tough.
11 Uncover, leave for another minute.
12 Serve with rice or noodles.

Grilling poultry

While a very young jointed duckling could be grilled, the most suitable poultry to choose is a young broiler chicken. Buy a bird which has already been jointed, or joint it yourself (see page 51). Cook as follows:

If wished, coat the joints with seasoned flour. Put the joints on to the greased grid of the grill pan, brush with plenty of oil or melted butter. Put under a hot grill – but not too near the heat. Grill quickly until the skin is golden brown, turn and brush the under side with more butter or oil, and continue browning.

Either move further away from the grill heat, or lower this and cook steadily until cooked through to the centre.

Mushrooms, tomatoes, etc., can either be put round the joints half way through cooking or can be cooked in the grill pan under the chicken. Use any juices that drop into the pan as the basis for a sauce if wished.

Grilled chicken with parsley butter

cooking time: 20 minutes

you will need:

grilled chicken	grated lemon rind
butter	chopped parsley

Cook the chicken as above, and serve with pats of butter flavoured with grated lemon rind and chopped parsley.

Curried grilled chicken

cooking time: 20 minutes

you will need:

jointed chicken	celery salt
flour	melted butter
curry powder	lemon wedges
cayenne pepper	

1 Sprinkle the joints of chicken with flour, mixed with little curry powder, cayenne pepper and celery salt.
2 Brush with melted butter, then roll again in curry flavoured flour.
3 Cook as grilled chicken.
4 Serve with wedges of lemon.

Variation:

Lemon grilled chicken – omit the curry powder and seasonings as previous recipe and blend the finely grated rind of 1–2 lemons with the flour. Add the juice of 1–2 lemons, pinch paprika and pinch salt to the butter at stage 2, and continue as the recipe.

Grilled chicken with golden sauce

cooking time: 20 minutes

you will need:

4 chicken joints	2 oz. melted butter

for sauce:

1 oz. butter	salt and pepper
1 oz. plain flour	2 hard-boiled eggs
½ pint milk	watercress, to garnish
1 egg yolk	

1 Brush chicken joints with melted butter, grill for 3 minutes on each side.
2 Reduce heat and grill for 8–10 minutes each side.
3 Make sauce by melting butter, stirring in flour, and adding milk.
4 Cook until sauce thickens and remove from heat.
5 Beat in the egg yolk, seasoning and the very finely chopped hard-boiled eggs.
6 Serve chicken with sauce poured over, garnished with watercress.

Variation:

Grilled chicken and creamed corn – follow the directions for the recipe above, but. omit the hard-boiled eggs from the sauce. Make the sauce to stage 4, add a medium can corn kernels or cooked corn kernels and heat, then continue as the rest of the recipe.

Devilled turkey legs

cooking time: 10–15 minutes

you will need:
1 leg or 2 drum sticks turkey (if bird is large*)

for coating:

3 oz. turkey fat	squeeze lemon juice
6 oz. breadcrumbs	1 tablespoon chutney
1–2 level teaspoons curry powder	pinch each of salt, pepper, mustard, sugar
½–1 teaspoon Worcestershire sauce	

*or if preferred, small thick pieces of turkey meat.

1 Mix all coating ingredients together.
2 Spread over pieces of turkey meat.
3 Brown on both sides under hot grill.
4 Lower heat and cook more slowly to heat through.
5 Serve with potatoes and peas.

Devilled chicken (1)

cooking time: 10–12 minutes

you will need:

12 oz. cold chicken	½ teaspoon black pepper
2 teaspoons tomato ketchup	2 teaspoons made mustard
2 teaspoons vinegar	2 tablespoons olive oil
pinch cayenne pepper	

1 Cut the chicken into neat pieces.
2 Blend all the other ingredients together.
3 Brush over the chicken.
4 Grill until browned on both sides.
5 Serve hot with boiled rice, vegetables and sweet chutney, or cold with salad.

Making terrines and loaves etc. with poultry and game

The following two recipes are basic ones for making a terrine and a loaf. They can however be varied according to the ingredients available. For example try duck instead of chicken in the terrine, mixing a little chopped sage with seasoning. Or use chicken instead of rabbit in the loaf, or grouse or pigeons.
Either of these recipes is an easy to serve and an economical way of using poultry and game. Also, because they can be carved so effortlessly, they are ideal for entertaining.

Chicken terrine

cooking time: 1¼–1¾ hours

you will need:

1 small chicken	seasoning
6 rashers streaky bacon or bacon pieces	1 tablespoon sherry (if desired)
	3 tablespoons stock

1 Cut the breast away from the bones, slicing this carefully.
2 Remove all the rest of the meat from the bones.
3 Put this, together with the giblets and bacon,

through a mincer, using all the skin; or chop the chicken meat, giblets and bacon very finely.

4 Grease a good sized basin or mould.
5 Put one third of the minced chicken at the bottom.
6 Cover this with half the sliced chicken breast, seasoning each layer well.
7 Continue with another third of the minced chicken, then the rest of the breast and finally the remainder of the minced chicken.
8 Mix the sherry with the chicken stock and seasoning.
9 Pour over the meat.
10 Cover with buttered paper and cook for approximately 1¼ hours in the centre of a very moderate oven (350°F. – Gas Mark 3). If the chicken is not very young, allow up to 1¾ hours.

Variation:

Game terrine – use 1 large pheasant, 2 grouse or 4 pigeons instead of the chicken in the recipe above. Use sherry as stage 8 or brandy.

Rabbit loaf

cooking time: 1–2 hours

you will need:

1 rabbit	3 tablespoons milk or
4 oz. bacon pieces	stock
1 oz. fat	little margarine
1 large onion	crisp breadcrumbs if
8 oz. pork sausage	baking or soft
meat	crumbs if steaming
seasoning	

1 Cut all the meat from the rabbit bones with a sharp knife and use these to give stock to serve with the rabbit loaf for a hot dish.
2 Put the rabbit flesh and bacon through a mincer. Fry the onion in the fat.
3 Add to the sausage meat and mince.
4 Other flavourings can be added if wished – chopped parsley, little sage, garlic or garlic salt, chopped celery or celery salt.
5 Blend and season well.
6 Gradually moisten with the milk or stock from simmering the bones with the liver of the rabbit.
7 Grease a mould or tin with the margarine and coat with the crumbs.
8 Put in the rabbit mixture, and cover with foil or greased paper.
9 Either steam for about 2 hours or bake for 1–1¼ hours, in the centre of a moderate oven (375°F. – Gas Mark 4).
10 Turn out and serve hot with gravy and mixed vegetables, or cold with salad.

Variation:

Chicken loaf – use a plump young chicken instead of the rabbit in previous recipe. Flavour with parsley, lemon and celery salt at stage 4.

To casserole poultry or game

The following recipes are meant primarily to tenderise rather older poultry or game, but each one can also be used as a basic recipe to adapt to other poultry or game. This method of cooking is ideal when entertaining, as it requires no last minute 'dishing up'. For such occasions, however, rather younger birds could be selected.

Devilled chicken (2)

cooking time: 1½–1¾ hours

you will need:

1 small young fowl (weighing about 2–2½ lb.)	1 teaspoon dry mustard
2–3 oz. margarine or oil	good pinch salt and pepper
½ teaspoon curry powder	1 dessertspoon lemon juice
1 tablespoon Worcestershire sauce	½ teaspoon sugar
little vinegar	2 oz. fine breadcrumbs

for sauce:

giblet stock	1 onion
seasoning	a little flour

1 First divide the uncooked fowl into neat joints.
2 Put the giblets into a saucepan, cover with water, add seasoning and the whole onion.
3 Cover the pan and simmer gently for good 30 minutes.
4 While these are simmering, prepare the chicken as follows: cream the margarine, add the curry powder, Worcestershire sauce, vinegar, mustard, salt, pepper, lemon juice and sugar.
5 Spread this paste over the joints of the chicken.
6 Roll in the soft breadcrumbs.
7 Grease a casserole thoroughly, put in the pieces of chicken and cover with any left-over crumbs, a piece of greased greaseproof paper, then lid of the casserole.
8 Bake for 1–1¼ hours in the middle of a very moderate oven (350°F. – Gas Mark 3).
9 During the cooking time take off the lid and add 2 tablespoons of the giblet stock if the chicken appears to be drying at all.
10 Put the cooked joints on a hot dish and pour round a sauce made by thickening the giblet stock with a little flour and cooking until smooth.

Country chicken

cooking time: 2–3 hours

you will need:

1 boiling fowl	1 pint water
2 oz. fat	pinch powdered thyme
2 oz. flour	squeeze lemon juice
seasoning	bay leaf
8 carrots	½ pint milk
3 onions	1–2 tablespoons cream

1 Cut the fowl into neat pieces. If large, make 9 joints (2 drum sticks, 2 thighs, 4 pieces breast and wing and the back). If small divide into 5 (halve breast and include wings on each side – leave thigh and drum sticks as one joint).
2 Heat fat in pan.
3 Flour the chicken with 1 oz. only of seasoned flour and toss in fat until pale gold.
4 Slice carrots and onions and add to the chicken, together with the giblets if wished.
5 Cover with water, add a little extra seasoning, the thyme, lemon juice and bay leaf.
6 Put lid on the pan and simmer for 2 hours with small bird, 3 hours with larger bird.
7 Remove bay leaf, blend rest of flour with the milk and add to stock.
8 Bring steadily to the boil and cook until thickened.
9 Stir in the cream.
10 Taste and reseason if wished.
11 Serve either with vegetables or to provide a contrast in texture, with orange salad and savoury scones.

Variation:

Country duck casserole – use the previous recipe for country chicken, but instead of milk use extra stock or cheap red wine, and omit the cream. Instead of carrots use about 8 oz. shelled chestnuts.

Boiled chicken

cooking time: 2½ hours

you will need:

boiling chicken (approximately 3 lb.)	2 small onions
2–3 sticks celery	¼ pint water
	seasoning

1 Simmer chicken with celery, onions, etc., for approximately 2½ hours until tender.
2 Serve with one of the following sauces:

White sauce – see recipe page 88, but use half chicken stock, and half milk.

Parsley sauce – see recipe page 88, but use half chicken stock, and half milk.

Hard-boiled egg sauce – see recipe page 88.

Turkey Creole

cooking time: 20–25 minutes

you will need:

4 oz. rice	¼ pint turkey stock
1 oz. turkey fat	about 12 oz. sliced
1 green pepper	cooked turkey meat
1 head celery (or can celery)	seasoning
	3 large tomatoes

1 Cook rice in boiling salted water.
2 Heat fat and toss in sliced pepper and large pieces of celery.
3 Add turkey stock.
4 Simmer until vegetables are nearly cooked.
5 Add turkey and season well.
6 When thoroughly hot, arrange on bed of cooked rice.
7 Garnish with sliced tomato.

Pigeon casserole

cooking time: 2¼ hours

you will need:

2 good sized pigeons	½ swede
1 oz. flour	½ pint stock
2 oz. fat	seasoning
1 onion	4 tomatoes
4 carrots	bay leaf

1 Fry the floured pigeons in the hot fat for a few minutes.
2 Lift out and put into a casserole.
3 Fry the chopped onion, carrots and diced swede in the fat and cook for a few minutes.
4 Gradually add the stock.
5 Bring to the boil and cook until thickened and smooth.
6 Season well.
7 Pour over the pigeons, adding the tomatoes, bay leaf and cover with a lid or foil.
8 Cook gently for about 2 hours in the centre of a very moderate oven (325°F.–350°F. – Gas Mark 2–3).
9 Remove bay leaf before serving.

Variations:

Grouse casserole – cook as for pigeon casserole above allowing 1 good sized grouse or 2 smaller ones. Diced bacon can be added if wished.

Casserole of hare – use a jointed young hare in

place of pigeons or grouse. Since this is larger (it would serve 6–8 people) double all the ingredients in previous recipe. Add a glass of port wine and 2 tablespoons redcurrant jelly to the sauce at stage 5.

Devilled rabbit

cooking time: 1½ hours

you will need:

1 rabbit	1 teaspoon Worcestershire sauce
little vinegar	
4 oz. fat bacon	1 pint water
large onion	seasoning
about 8 oz. diced mixed root vegetables	1 oz. flour
	¼ pint milk
	chopped parsley
1 teaspoon curry powder	

1 Wash the rabbit in cold water, to which a little vinegar is added to whiten the flesh.
2 Cut the meat into pieces.
3 Dice the bacon and put into a pan with chopped onion, vegetables, rabbit, curry powder and sauce.
4 Fry for a few minutes, then add water and bring to the boil.
5 Season well.
6 Put on the lid and simmer gently for about 1½ hours until the rabbit is tender.
7 Blend the flour with the milk and stir into the liquid.
8 Bring to the boil, stirring well and cook until smooth and thickened.
9 Taste and reseason if necessary.
10 Garnish with chopped parsley.

Jugged rabbit

cooking time: 2¼–3 hours

you will need:

1 rabbit	*bouquet garni*
1½ oz. clarified dripping	1 pint stock
1 oz. flour	salt and pepper
1 onion	8 peppercorns
2 cloves	1 oz. butter
¼ pint claret (optional)	1 scant oz. flour
1 teaspoon lemon juice	veal stuffing (see page 88)

to serve:
redcurrant jelly

1 Wash and dry rabbit, divide into joints and fry in hot fat until browned, sprinkling with the flour.
2 Add onion stuck with cloves, claret, lemon juice, *bouquet garni* and stock to cover.
3 Season with salt and peppercorns.
4 Cover and simmer for 2½–3 hours.
5 30 minutes before serving, thicken the sauce with 1 oz. butter worked with a little less flour and add more wine if desired for a fuller flavour.
6 Veal stuffing makes a good garnish and redcurrant jelly should be served separately.

Variation:
Jugged hare – this is almost more delicious than rabbit. Since the hare is larger you will need slightly more ingredients for the sauce, so use: 1½ pints stock at stage 2 with just over ¼ pint claret (or port wine). When thickening the sauce at stage 5, use 1½ oz. butter and 1½ oz. flour.

Rich rabbit stew

cooking time: 1¾–2¼ hours

you will need:

1 rabbit	*bouquet garni* (parsley, thyme, bay leaf)
4 oz. streaky bacon	
18 button onions	
2 oz. butter	3–4 cloves
1½ oz. flour	6 peppercorns
1 pint stock	salt
	¼ pint claret (optional)

1 Divide rabbit into small joints, dice the bacon, peel the onions.
2 Fry onions and bacon in butter until brown, and set aside.
3 Fry rabbit joints until lightly browned, add flour and cook until joints are well browned.
4 Replace onions and bacon, and add hot stock, *bouquet garni*, cloves, peppercorns and salt to taste.
5 Cover closely and simmer until rabbit is tender (approximately 1½–2 hours).
6 Shortly before serving add the claret and the rabbit liver finely chopped, letting it simmer for 10 minutes before serving.

Pressure Cooking of Meat, Poultry and Game

A pressure cooker is an excellent means of producing a first class meal in a remarkably short time. It also enables you to make the tougher and cheaper variety of meats and poultry really tender without having to cook them for hours. However, when using a pressure cooker, do remember the following points:

1 Do NOT allow longer cooking time than given in the recipes, since a few minutes in a pressure cooker corresponds to a considerably longer period of ordinary cooking.
2 Make sure the pieces of meat, poultry, etc. are cut to a uniform size.

Goulash

pressure cooking time: 20–25 minutes

you will need:

1 lb. stewing meat (preferably beef)	¼ pint stock or water seasoning (include
1 oz. fat	1–2 teaspoons
1 medium sized onion	paprika pepper)
¼ pint tomato pulp or canned tomatoes	1 lb. potatoes

1 Cut the meat into neat cubes.
2 Heat the fat at the bottom of the cooker and fry the meat and onion until brown.
3 Add tomato pulp, stock, seasoning and paprika.
4 Fix the lid and bring to pressure.
5 Allow pressure to drop then add the sliced potatoes.
6 Re-fix the lid, and bring once again to pressure.
7 Lower the heat and cook for 10 minutes.

Note: This should be a very thick stew.

Oxtail

pressure cooking time: 20 minutes

you will need:

1 oxtail	1 stick celery
1 oz. dripping	seasoning
¾ pint water	4 cloves (optional)
2 onions	1 oz. flour
2 carrots	parsley, to garnish

1 Cut the oxtail into sections.
2 Melt the dripping in bottom of the cooker and fry oxtail until just brown.
3 Add the water, vegetables, seasoning and cloves.

4 Fix the lid, bring to pressure.
5 Then lower the heat.
6 Cook for 20–25 minutes.
7 Allow pressure to drop then remove the lid.
8 Blend the flour with a little cold water or stock.
9 Add to the liquid and bring to the boil.
10 Boil until thick.
11 Serve sprinkled with parsley.

Galantine of rabbit

pressure cooking time: 15 minutes at 15 lb. pressure

cooking time: 1¾–2 hours

you will need:

1 medium sized rabbit	vegetables for making stock (optional)
2 tomatoes	milk or stock to bind
½ teaspoon chopped or powdered dried sage	
½ teaspoon grated lemon rind	**to coat:** little flour
1 egg	1 teaspoon breadcrumbs
seasoning	

1 Remove all the meat from the bones.
2 Put the meat, including liver and heart of rabbit through a mincer.
3 Mix the rabbit meat with all other ingredients, skinning tomatoes and chopping them finely.
4 Add just enough milk or stock (made from rabbit bones) to make a sticky consistency.
5 Form into a roll, flouring the outside lightly.
6 Put either into greased paper, a floured cloth or greased mould.
7 Put ½ pint water into the pressure cooker, then stand the galantine on the rack.
8 Bring rapidly to pressure, then maintain at pressure for 15 minutes.
9 Allow pressure to drop gradually.
10 Coat the galantine with crisp breadcrumbs.
11 If preferred, steam for 1¾–2 hours.

To make stock:

1 Put the rabbit bones with seasoning into the cooker just covering them with water.
2 Vegetables, such as sliced onion or carrot, can be added if wished. Do not use rack.
3 Bring the cooker to pressure, then maintain at pressure, for 20 minutes.

Braised heart

pressure cooking time: 25 minutes

you will need:

1 lb. ox heart or sheep heart	bunch herbs or 1 teaspoon mixed herbs
1 oz. dripping	½ pint stock, **or** water flavoured with meat **or** vegetables extract
2 onions	
2 carrots	
1 small turnip	1 oz. flour plus little extra flour for coating
seasoning	

1 Cut ox heart into thick slices.
2 Heat fat in bottom of pressure cooker.
3 Flour the hearts and season well.
4 Fry in the hot fat until brown.
5 Add all the other ingredients, except the 1 oz. flour.
6 Fix the lid and bring to pressure.
7 Lower heat and cook for 25 minutes.
8 Blend the flour with very little cold stock.
9 Add to the liquid.
10 Bring to the boil and boil for 3 minutes.

Savoury Pies and Puddings

Baking meat or poultry in a pastry crust or in a steamed or boiled pudding helps to retain much of the flavour. Whenever possible, do NOT pre-cook meat, although in some recipes this is essential.

Hot water crust pastry (or raised pastry)

cooking time: according to recipe

you will need:

12 oz. plain flour	3–4 oz. fat
pinch salt	¼ pint water

1 Sieve flour and salt.
2 Melt fat in warm water and add to flour.
3 Mix with knife and knead gently with fingers.

Note: Unlike other pastry, this should be used when warm.

Beef flan

cooking time: 25–30 minutes

you will need:

6 oz. short crust pastry (see page 75)	or 1 can stewing steak or steak and vegetables and 1 teaspoon cornflour to thicken liquid from can
either 8 oz. diced, cooked meat **or** flaked corn beef	
¼ pint **thick** brown sauce or tomato sauce (see pages 87, 88)	

to garnish:

3 skinned tomatoes	1–2 hard-boiled eggs

1 Bake pastry in flan case 'blind' until crisp and golden.
2 Heat the meat and liquid together, blending in the cornflour, if necessary.
3 Garnish with sliced tomatoes and hard-boiled egg or eggs, arranging these alternately round the flan.
4 Serve hot or cold. If serving hot, wait until meat mixture is very hot, then pour into hot flan and garnish. Do not heat together, otherwise the pastry becomes soggy.
  For a cold flan, put cold meat mixture into cold cooked pastry case and garnish.

Croustade of beef

cooking time: 45 minutes–1 hour

you will need:

4–6 oz. short crust pastry (see page 75)	approximately 1 lb. fillet rump or other grilling steak CUT IN ONE PIECE
2–3 oz. mushrooms	
1 oz. butter	
seasoning	

1 Roll out the pastry very thinly to a neat oblong.
2 Chop the mushrooms finely and blend with the butter and seasoning to form an almost paste-like consistency.
3 Spread this over the centre of the pastry, leaving the ends quite bare.
4 Put the piece of steak on top, season lightly and wrap it up in the pastry dough.
5 Tuck in the ends and seal the edges with water.
6 Put on to a lightly greased baking tin.
7 If you like it rare, allow 20–25 minutes in a hot

oven (475°F. – Gas Mark 8), then lower the heat to moderate and allow a further 20 minutes.

If you like it medium, when the heat is lowered to moderate allow 30–40 minutes.

If you like it well done, allow a good 40 minutes after turning down to moderate.

8 Serve with mushroom sauce or brown sauce (see page 88).

Variation:

Lamb cushions – use lean lamb chops in place of steak. Make up 8 oz. pastry to cover 4 good sized lamb chops. Roll out the pastry and cut into 4 squares, then continue as the recipe to the end of stage 3. Cook the chops for 15 minutes and cool. Put on the pastry, wrap carefully, then bake as stage 7.

Hasty steak pie

6 servings

cooking time: 45 minutes

you will need:

6 oz. short crust pastry (see page 75)	2 tomatoes
1 oz. butter	1 16-oz. can stewed steak
1 onion	1 packet peanuts (optional)
1 green pepper	

1 Divide pastry in half.
2 Roll out one piece and line an 8-inch pie dish.
3 Melt butter in saucepan.
4 Chop onions and pepper finely and fry in butter.
5 Chop tomatoes and add them when onion has just started to turn colour.
6 Add can of steak and mix all ingredients well together.
7 Transfer into pastry case when cool.
8 Roll out remaining pastry and cover pie, marking edge with a fork.
9 Prick top, brush with a little milk and toss peanuts onto it.
10 Bake in centre of a hot oven (425°F. – Gas Mark 6) for 30–35 minutes.

Meat and vegetable roll

cooking time: 1 hour

you will need:

8 oz. plain flour	8 oz. minced beef
2 level teaspoons baking powder	1 finely chopped carrot and onion
pinch salt	salt and pepper
1½ oz. margarine or lard	2 tablespoons stock
cold water to mix	milk to glaze

1 Sieve together plain flour, baking powder and salt.
2 Rub in fat until mixture resembles breadcrumbs.
3 Add sufficient cold water to give a dry dough.
4 Mix together minced beef, finely chopped carrot and onion.
5 Season well with salt and pepper.
6 Add stock to moisten.
7 Roll pastry out to a large rectangle and trim edges.
8 Cover with filling, leaving ½-inch pastry edge.
9 Brush this with a little water and roll up as for Swiss roll.
10 Seal ends, prick the top with a fork and decorate with pastry leaves.
11 Brush with a little milk and bake in a moderately hot oven (400°F. – Gas Mark 5) for 1 hour.
12 Serve with chipped potatoes and a green vegetable.

Lamb pies

cooking time: 1¼ hours

you will need:

8 oz. lamb	1 dessertspoon thick gravy
1 small onion, finely chopped	seasoning
½ oz. dripping	6 oz. short crust pastry (see page 75)
1 tablespoon parsley	little beaten egg
1 dessertspoon tomato ketchup	

1 Mince the lamb.
2 Fry onion lightly in the melted dripping and add to the meat, parsley, ketchup and gravy.
3 Season well.
4 Line deep patty tins with rounds of pastry and damp edges.
5 Fill with the meat mixture and cover with a second round of pastry.
6 Seal and crimp the edges and make a small slit in the top to allow steam to escape.
7 Decorate if liked and brush with beaten egg.
8 Bake in a moderate oven (375°F. – Gas Mark 4) for 25 minutes.
9 Reduce heat to a slower oven (300°F. – Gas Mark 2) and cook for a further 1 hour.

Variation:

With cooked lamb – if liked this recipe can be made using cooked lamb, in which case the cooking time is 25 minutes in a moderate oven (375°F. – Gas Mark 4).

Lamb slices

cooking time: 1 hour

you will need:

8 oz. short crust pastry (see page 75)	2 tomatoes
12 oz. fresh lamb	1 oz. dripping or lard
2 onions	pinch chopped mint
	seasoning

1 Roll out the pastry to a neat oblong shape.
2 Mince or chop the lamb finely.
3 Chop and fry the onions and tomatoes in the hot dripping until very soft.
4 Mix with the lamb, add mint, seasoning.
5 Spread over pastry.
6 Roll like a Swiss roll, then bake in the centre of a hot oven (425°F.–450°F. – Gas Mark 6–7) for approximately 25 minutes.
7 Lower the heat to moderate (375°F. – Gas Mark 4) for a further 30–40 minutes.
8 Cut into slices and serve hot or cold.

Variation:

Beef slices – use 12 oz. canned corned beef in place of lamb. Flake this and mix with the ingredients as stages 3 and 4. A more appropriate flavouring for beef is chopped parsley and a little made mustard, so omit the mint.

Mutton pie

cooking time: 2 hours

you will need:

8 small mutton cutlets	8 small tomatoes
8 small onions	few capers
2 oz. fat	6 oz. flaky or short crust pastry (see page 75)
1 oz. flour	
¾ pint water	
seasoning	

1 Brown meat then onions in the fat.
2 Stir in the flour and cook for a few minutes.
3 Add water, bring to the boil and stir until smooth.
4 Season well.
5 Put lid on pan and simmer for 1 hour.
6 Lift onions and meat out of stock.
7 Arrange in pie dish so that all the bones are standing upright in the centre of the dish.
8 Put in tomatoes, capers and some of the gravy.
9 Cover with pastry, allowing bones to pierce this in the centre.
10 Bake for approximately 45 minutes in a really hot oven, then reduce heat for 20–25 minutes.

Meat and egg pasty

cooking time: 45 minutes

you will need:

for pastry:

8 oz. plain flour	2 oz. lard
½ teaspoon salt	2 oz. butter
½ teaspoon baking powder	4 tablespoons cold water

for filling:

1 can corned beef	4 eggs
½ pint can mushroom soup	

1 Firstly, make the pastry. Sieve the dry ingredients.
2 Rub in the fat and butter until mixture is crumbly.
3 Mix to a soft dough with water.
4 Divide into 2 pieces and roll out.
5 Line a 7- or 7½-inch ovenproof dish (1½–2 inches deep) with 1 piece of pastry.
6 Make the filling – open the can of corned beef and tip into a bowl.
7 Mash with a fork and stir in half the mushroom soup.
8 Put mixture into the dish.
9 Make 4 hollows in the meat mixture and drop an unbeaten egg into each.
10 Carefully cover with the rest of the meat. If possible keep the yolks whole, but if they break it doesn't matter.
11 Cover with pastry, neaten edges and decorate.
12 Bake for 45 minutes in a moderately hot oven (400°F. – Gas Mark 5).
13 Heat rest of soup and serve as a sauce.

Veal and ham pie

cooking time: 2¼ hours

you will need:

12 oz. raised pastry (see page 58)	7 tablespoons water or bone stock
1 lb. fillet veal	beaten eggs for glazing
6 oz. ham	1 level teaspoon gelatine
salt and pepper	½ level teaspoon meat extract
½ level teaspoon grated lemon rind	
1–2 hard-boiled eggs	

1 Make pastry and keep warm in basin until ready to use.
2 Remove pastry from basin and with two-thirds of the dough line a 6-inch cake tin or 1 lb. loaf tin.

3 Wash and dry the meats, removing any skin, and cut into 1-inch cubes.

4 Roll the meat together in salt and pepper and lemon rind.

5 Place half the meat in the bottom of the pastry-lined tin.

6 Cut the eggs into halves.

7 Place on top of the meat and cover with remaining meat.

8 Pour into the pie 3 tablespoons of the water or stock.

9 Turn the top edges of pastry lining in over the meat, damp it all around.

10 Roll out the remaining third of pastry to make a lid.

11 Press down well all round edges and cut at ½ inch intervals with a sharp knife to secure.

12 Make a hole in the centre, brush over with beaten egg, decorate with pastry 'leaves' and again brush with beaten egg.

13 Place in the centre of a moderate oven (375°F. – Gas Mark 4) for 2–2¼ hours.

14 Leave to cool.

15 Melt the gelatine in remaining water or stock and stir in the meat extract.

16 When the pie is cool and the gelatine mixture just setting, pour into the pie through the hole in the centre.

17 Leave to set before serving.

Variations:

Chicken and ham pie No. 1 – use about 1 lb. diced raw chicken instead of veal. Have half light and half dark meat to give a variety of flavour.

Pork pie – use 1½ lb. lean pork (cut from the leg of pork) instead of veal and ham. Omit the hard-boiled eggs, if wished.

Ulster flan

cooking time: 1 hour

you will need:

for pastry:

6 oz. plain flour, sifted	salt
3 oz. butter	1 oz. grated cheese

for filling:

6 oz. bacon, streaky or back	salt and pepper
bare ¼ pint milk	2 large eggs

1 Make the pastry by rubbing butter into the flour and salt.

2 Add the cheese and mix with water until normal pastry consistency is obtained.

3 Roll out, line an 8-inch flan ring with it, then bake blind (see page 74) for approximately 20 minutes, until pale golden brown.

4 Prepare the filling. First remove bacon rind.

5 Cut up the bacon, lightly grill or fry and put into the pastry case.

6 Add milk and seasonings to the beaten eggs.

7 Strain into the pastry case.

8 Bake in very moderate oven (350°F. – Gas Mark 3) for about 40 minutes.

Chicken and bacon pie

cooking time: 2 hours for chicken, 45 minutes for pie

you will need:

small boiling fowl, or half a large one (with giblets)	2 hard-boiled eggs
seasoning	⅓ pint chicken stock
pinch mixed herbs	6–8 oz. short crust or flaky pastry (see page 75)
little lemon rind	
2–3 rashers bacon or piece ham	

1 Simmer the fowl until tender. Cook giblets as well.

2 When cooking add seasoning, pinch mixed herbs and lemon rind.

3 Remove meat from bone and cut into small pieces.

4 Mix the light and dark meat together with the giblets.

5 Chop the uncooked bacon into small pieces.

6 Slice the hard-boiled eggs.

7 Season meat well.

8 Put a layer of chicken meat, then egg and bacon into pie dish, fill like this.

9 Cover with chicken stock.

10 Put on pastry lid and bake for about 45 minutes in centre of oven. Start with hot oven (425°F.–445°F. – Gas Mark 6–7) then lower to moderate (375°F. – Gas Mark 4).

11 Serve hot or cold.

Variations:

With potato – mashed potatoes could be used instead of pastry for the pie.

With beef – beef, simmered gently, could be used instead of chicken; add sliced tomatoes and mushrooms as well as the bacon.

Chicken and ham pie No. (2)

cooking time: approximately 1½ hours

you will need:

for hot water crust pastry:

scant ¼ pint water
4 oz. cooking fat or lard
large pinch salt
10 oz. flour (with plain flour 1½ level teaspoons baking powder)

1 Put water, lard and salt into pan.
2 Heat together until lard has dissolved.
3 Pour over the flour, knead well, use while warm and keep warm.

for filling:

small cooked boiling fowl or ½ larger fowl
bay leaf
seasoning
pinch mixed herbs
4 oz. bacon or cooked ham
egg or milk, to glaze
1 teaspoon powdered gelatine
3 tablespoons chicken stock plus stock to moisten

1 Cut all the bones away from the chicken and simmer these with bay leaf, seasoning and herbs.
2 Dice the chicken meat and ham and mix together keeping the stock separately.
3 Make a round or oval of pastry and long strip and line the bottom and sides of a 6 or 7-inch tin, fill with chicken mixture and a very little stock.
4 Make a round of pastry to cover the filling.
5 Lay this on top, it is important to seal the edges firmly.
6 Do not press down the pastry too hard since there must be room to pour in the jellied stock after cooking.
7 Make a slit in the centre of the top pastry and use any pieces left to form leaves, a rose or tassel.
8 Brush with the milk or beaten egg and milk to glaze the pie.
9 Bake for about 1¼–1½ hours in the centre of a moderately hot oven (400°F. – Gas Mark 5). If the pie is becoming too brown reduce heat slightly.
10 Allow to cool before removing from tin. Or if you have a special raised pie tin, unlock this carefully.
11 When the pie is cool, fill with the jellied stock.
12 To make this, dissolve the powdered gelatine in the 3 tablespoons chicken stock and pour through the split in the top of the pie.
13 Make a small greaseproof paper funnel for easy pouring.

Picnic roll

cooking time: 1 hour

you will need:

1 onion
1½ oz. butter
1 oz. flour
¼ pint milk
12 oz. minced cooked chicken, veal or beef
4 oz. chopped or minced ham
2–3 tablespoons breadcrumbs
seasoning
2–3 hard-boiled eggs
8–10 oz. short crust pastry (see page 75)
egg or milk, to glaze

1 Chop the onion and fry in the butter.
2 Stir in the flour.
3 Cook for several minutes.
4 Remove from heat and add milk.
5 Bring to boil, cook until very thick.
6 Add the veal or chicken, ham, crumbs and seasoning.
7 Press mixture on to floured board and form into oblong shape.
8 Put eggs on this then mould mixture round them. Form into a neat roll.
9 Roll out pastry into oblong shape.
10 Lift meat and egg roll onto this – wrap up in a neat parcel sealing top and ends.
11 Lift on to greased baking tin with sealed side on tin.
12 Slit along top to allow steam to escape. Brush with egg and milk or milk and bake for 40 minutes in centre of moderately hot oven (400°F. – Gas Mark 5).

Variation:

Seafood roll – use flaked canned tuna or salmon in place of the chicken or beef and ham. Flavour with the grated rind and juice of 1 lemon at stage 6.

Turkey vol-au-vent

cooking time: 35 minutes

you will need:

8 oz. turkey pieces from carcase and wings
4 oz. mushrooms
1 oz. butter
1 oz. flour
¼ pint stock or milk
salt and pepper
8 oz. puff pastry
egg, to glaze

1 Cut the turkey off the bones and divide into evenly sized pieces.
2 Wash and slice the mushrooms.

3 Melt the butter in a saucepan and add the flour.

4 Pour in the stock, bring to the boil and stir until the sauce is thick.

5 Add the pieces of turkey and the mushrooms and heat gently for 5 minutes. Season.

6 In the meantime, roll out the pastry and cut into a large round. With a small cutter or saucer press a circle into the middle of the pastry, pressing half way through pastry.

7 Glaze the top and sides with a little beaten egg.

8 Bake in centre of very hot oven (475°F. – Gas Mark 8) for 10 minutes, then lower heat to moderately hot (400°F. – Gas Mark 5) for 10–12 minutes.

9 Carefully cut off the lid of the vol-au-vent and remove the dough.

10 Return the shell and the lid to the oven to dry out for 5–8 minutes.

11 Fill the shell with the hot turkey mixture and replace the lid.

12 Serve immediately.

Variation:

Game vol-au-vent – use cooked game in place of turkey. Either heat in a white sauce as the recipe above or make a brown sauce instead. Add the mushrooms and game to this sauce, flavour with a little brandy or sherry.

Turkey pie

cooking time: 35 minutes

you will need:

short crust pastry (see page 75)	scant ¼ pint turkey stock (made by simmering giblets)
12 oz. cooked turkey meat	1 hard-boiled egg
4 oz. bacon	1 egg yolk
seasoning	1 teaspoon powder gelatine

1 Roll out pastry and line deep oval, round or square tin with two-thirds of it.

2 Arrange sliced meat and bacon in this, adding seasoning and about 1 dessertspoon only of stock.

3 Place hard-boiled egg in centre.

4 Cover with pastry and decorate with pastry leaves. Do not press pastry 'lid' down too tightly on to meat.

5 Brush with beaten egg yolk.

6 Cook for about 25 minutes in centre of hot oven (425°F.–450°F. – Gas Mark 6–7), then lower heat to moderate (375°F. – Gas Mark 4) for further 10 minutes.

7 Cool slightly and turn out of tin.

8 If sides are not really brown, put into oven on flat baking tray for few minutes.

9 Allow pie to cool again.

10 Meanwhile, dissolve gelatine in turkey stock, allowing this to become quite cold and slightly stiffened.

11 Then pour through hole in top of pie.

Steak and liver pudding

cooking time: 4–5 hours

you will need:
for the pastry:

8 oz. plain flour	4 oz. suet (chopped finely)
1 level teaspoon baking powder	cold water to mix
little salt	

for filling:

1 lb. stewing steak	chopped onion (optional)
4 oz. liver	beef stock or cold water
flour, seasoned with salt and pepper	

1 Sieve together plain flour, baking powder and salt.

2 Mix in suet and bring to a stiff paste with cold water.

3 Knead slightly.

4 Cut off one third of pastry and retain for pudding lid.

5 Roll out remaining pastry into a circle ⅛ inch thick.

6 Line a greased 2-pint basin with this.

7 Cut steak into cubes, slice liver and coat each piece with seasoned flour.

8 Turn meat into lined basin.

9 Add a chopped onion to meat if desired.

10 Add enough stock or water to come half way up the meat.

11 Roll out pastry for top and seal onto pastry in basin.

12 Cover with foil or paper and steam for 4–5 hours.

Mushroom steak and kidney pudding

cooking time: 4–6 hours

you will need:

1 lb. beef steak, shin, blade or chuck	8 oz. suet crust pastry (see page 76)
8 oz. ox kidney	½ oz. butter
1 oz. seasoned flour	little water or stock
4 oz. mushrooms	

1 Cut the steak into small cubes.
2 Wash, skin and cut the kidney into similar sized cubes, removing the core.
3 Roll in the well seasoned flour.
4 Wash and chop the mushrooms.
5 Make suet crust pastry.
6 Line buttered basin with suet crust pastry.
7 Fill the basin with the steak, kidney and mushrooms and pour in sufficient water or stock to come three-quarters of the way up.
8 Put the dough lid on top and seal to the lining with water.
9 Cover first with greaseproof paper, then with foil, and tie down covers securely.
10 Steam for 4–6 hours.
11 Turn out carefully.

Mutton pudding

cooking time: 4–5 hours

you will need:

8–10 oz. suet crust pastry (see page 76)	8 pieces scrag end neck mutton
little flour	8 small onions
seasoning	2 lambs' kidneys

1 Line basin with suet crust pastry rolling this out thinly and keeping back enough for a lid.
2 Fill with floured and seasoned meat, onions, chopped kidney and water to come two-thirds up basin.
3 Put on a suet pastry 'lid' and seal edges. Cover with greased paper, foil or a cloth. Steam or boil for about 4–5 hours.

Variation:

Chicken and vegetable pudding – choose a small boiling fowl, and cut this into joints. Remove bones if possible and roll the chicken meat in well-seasoned flour, at stage 2. Put into the lined basin with 2 oz. button mushrooms, the onions and 2–3 sliced raw carrots. Add water or use chicken stock (made by simmering the giblets in salted water) as stage 2, continue as recipe.

Vegetable and Salad Dishes

A well planned vegetable dish can be served as a main course, particularly if used in conjunction with cheese, or a small amount of meat or poultry. Take advantage of the more unusual vegetables, and try serving them with satisfying sauces or stuffings as your main dish. Many of the following recipes are suitable for this sort of meal.

Stuffed aubergines

cooking time: 1 hour

you will need:

4 aubergines	chopped parsley
1 small onion	1 egg
1 tablespoon olive oil	¼ pint hot water
4 oz. minced beef	1 meat extract cube
1 oz. breadcrumbs	

to serve: tomato sauce (see page 87)

1 Halve the aubergines – remove centre pulp and mix it with chopped onion.
2 Fry onion and centre pulp in olive oil.
3 Add meat, breadcrumbs, parsley, egg, water and meat cube.
4 Fill the aubergines with the mixture and place on a greased baking dish.
5 Bake for about 1 hour in a moderate oven (375°F. – Gas Mark 4).
6 Serve with tomato sauce.

Stuffed sweet peppers or capsicums

cooking time: 1 hour

you will need:

3–4 peppers
1 small onion
1 tablespoon olive oil
4 oz. minced beef
1 oz. breadcrumbs

1 egg
chopped parsley
¼ pint hot water
1 meat extract cube

to serve:

tomato sauce (see page 87)

1 Cut peppers in half and remove seeds.
2 Fry chopped onion in olive oil.
3 Add meat, breadcrumbs, egg, parsley, water and meat cube.
4 Fill the peppers with the mixture and place on a greased baking dish.
5 Bake for about 45 minutes in a moderate oven (375°F. – Gas Mark 4).
6 Serve with tomato sauce.

Stuffed marrow

cooking time: 1¼ hours

you will need:

small marrow
1 small onion
1 tablespoon olive oil
4 oz. minced beef
1 oz. breadcrumbs

1 egg
chopped parsley
¼ pint hot water
1 meat extract cube

to serve:

tomato sauce (see page 87)

1 Halve marrow lengthways, remove seeds.
2 Fry chopped onion in olive oil.
3 Add meat, breadcrumbs, egg, parsley, water and meat cube.
4 Fill each half of marrow with the mixture and place on a greased baking dish.
5 Bake in a hot oven for about an hour.
6 Serve with tomato sauce.

Variation:

Stuffed green peppers – use the recipe above as a stuffing in green peppers. Halve large peppers, remove core and seeds and simmer peppers in boiling, salted water for 5 minutes. Drain and cool and pack with the stuffing. Bake on a greased dish for approximately 35 minutes in a hot oven.

Stuffed onions

pressure cooking time: 6 minutes

cooking time: 1½ hours

you will need:

4 medium sized Spanish onions
3 tablespoons breadcrumbs
1 oz. grated cheese

1 egg
1 oz. margarine or butter
seasoning

to serve:

white or cheese sauce (see page 88)

1 Wash the onions and remove the outer skins.
2 Put on the rack in the cooker with ¼ pint water and salt.
3 Fix the lid and bring to pressure.
4 Lower the heat and cook for 2 minutes.
5 Reduce the pressure immediately and open the cooker.
6 Take out the onions. These will not be cooked, but it will be possible to remove the centre core.
7 Chop this part of the onion finely.
8 Add to the other ingredients and pile this stuffing back into the centre cavity.
9 Put the onions into a greased container and stand on the rack with the same liquid.
10 Re-fix the lid and bring to pressure again.
11 Lower the heat and cook for a further 4 minutes.
12 Allow pan to return to normal pressure gradually.
13 Serve with white or cheese sauce.
14 This dish can also be cooked in an ordinary casserole for 1½ hours.

Vegetable pie

cooking time: 50 minutes

you will need:

1 lb. mixed diced vegetables
hard-boiled eggs (optional)

½ pint cheese sauce (see page 88)
1 lb. mashed potatoes
1 tablespoon grated cheese

1 Put the vegetables into a greased pie dish.
2 If using hard-boiled eggs, slice and arrange on top of vegetables.
3 Pour over the sauce and cover with the mashed potato.
4 Sprinkle on the grated cheese and bake for 30 minutes in the centre of a moderately hot oven (400°F. – Gas Mark 5) until crisp and brown.

Summer casserole au gratin

cooking time: 35–40 minutes

you will need:

8 oz. cooked young carrots	about 12 spring onions
1–2 cooked diced turnips	2 oz. butter
4–6 cooked diced new potatoes	2–3 tomatoes

for sauce:

1½ oz. butter	2 eggs
1½ oz. flour	seasoning
½ pint milk	3 oz. grated cheese

Toss all the vegetables in the butter, except the tomatoes, which should be sliced and added afterwards.

2 Put into casserole.

3 Make thick sauce of butter, flour, milk; add egg yolks and seasoning, the grated cheese, and stiffly beaten egg whites.

4 Pour over vegetables and put into centre of moderately hot oven (400°F. – Gas Mark 5) for about 25 minutes until well risen and firm.

A summer salad sandwich

cooking time: 25–30 minutes

you will need:

for cheese scone mixture:

8 oz. plain flour	pinch pepper
½ level teaspoon salt	1½ oz. butter
½ level teaspoon dry mustard	8 oz. grated Cheddar cheese
1 level teaspoon baking powder	scant ¼ pint ice cold water

for filling:

2 oz. butter	2 level teaspoons anchovy paste
1 rounded teaspoon chopped capers	3 tomatoes cucumber

1 Sieve dry ingredients into a large bowl, rub in butter and mix in cheese.

2 Mix to a stiff dough with ice cold water, knead slightly and turn onto floured board.

3 Form into oblong and roll to ½ inch thickness.

4 Wrap dough in greaseproof paper and enclose in aluminium foil.

5 Store in chill tray of refrigerator until required.

6 Cut dough into six fingers, place on baking sheet and bake in a hot oven (425°F. – Gas Mark 6) for 25–30 minutes, until golden brown.

7 Cool on a rack.

8 When cold split each scone in three.

9 For the filling cream butter and beat in capers and anchovy paste.

10 Spread bottom layer of scones with anchovy butter.

11 Place middle layer on top and cover with sliced tomatoes or cucumber.

12 Cover with top layer of scone and garnish with slices of tomato or cucumber.

Cheese and plum salad

no cooking

you will need:

1 lb. ripe plums	good pinch cinnamon
4 oz. grated Cheddar cheese	lettuce leaves
2 level teaspoons mayonnaise	watercress

1 Wash and dry plums; cut in half and remove stones.

2 To make filling, mix grated cheese, mayonnaise and cinnamon to soft paste and form into small balls, allowing one ball to each plum.

3 Sandwich filling and plums together and stand on a bed of lettuce.

4 Garnish with watercress.

Variations:

Cheese and apricot salad – use the same filling for well-drained, canned apricots, or for ripe halved apricots.

Cheese and apple ring salad – core, but do not peel dessert apples, sprinkle either with lemon juice or an oil and vinegar dressing. Put on a bed of lettuce, then top with balls of the cheese mixture and garnish with dates or walnuts.

Moulded chicken salad

cooking time: few minutes

you will need:

about 1 lb. cooked chicken or chicken and ham
1 pint chicken stock or use can chicken soup and make up to 1 pint with milk or water
1 oz. gelatine
3 tablespoons mayonnaise
2 hard-boiled eggs
3–4 oz. cooked diced vegetables, peas, carrots, cucumbers, etc.
seasoning
lettuce, tomatoes

1 Chop chicken fairly finely, but do not mince.
2 Heat most of the chicken stock.
3 Soften gelatine in remaining liquid.
4 Add to hot stock and stir until thoroughly dissolved.
5 Cool, then stir in chicken, mayonnaise, chopped eggs, vegetables and seasoning.
6 Pour into mould or basin and leave to set.
7 Serve with lettuce and tomatoes.

Salmon cream

cooking time: 10 minutes

you will need:

¼ pint aspic jelly
1 level teaspoon powdered gelatine
¼ pint mayonnaise
2 tablespoons cream
8–12 oz. cooked salmon
2 hard-boiled eggs
2 sliced gherkins
seasoning

1 When making the aspic jelly, dissolve the extra teaspoon gelatine powder in the liquid.
2 Allow to cool.
3 Mix with the mayonnaise, cream, flaked salmon and 1 of the chopped hard-boiled eggs and 1 of the gherkins.
4 Season well.
5 Put into a rinsed mould and allow to set.
6 Turn out and decorate with the other egg and gherkin. Serve with salad.

Tossed cheese salad

no cooking

you will need:

2 medium sized onions
2 large tomatoes
1 small lettuce
1 bunch watercress
few chives
8 oz. diced Cheddar cheese
1 tablespoon olive oil
1 tablespoon vinegar
salt and pepper
1 teaspoon lemon juice

1 Slice onions thinly and cut tomatoes in 8 pieces.
2 Shred lettuce coarsely.
3 Place in salad bowl with half watercress, tomatoes, chopped chives and cheese.
4 Whisk olive oil in vinegar a little at a time with seasoning and lemon juice.
5 Pour over salad ingredients and toss well.
6 Arrange sliced onion around edge of bowl and place remaining watercress in a bunch in centre. Chill for 30 minutes before serving.

Orange salad (to serve with cold duck, goose, etc.)

no cooking

you will need:

lettuce
2 large oranges
small teaspoon mustard
good pinch salt, pepper and sugar
1½ tablespoons oil
1½ tablespoons vinegar

1 Wash and dry lettuce and arrange on small plates.
2 Peel oranges and remove outside pith.
3 Then, using a very sharp knife, cut sections from the oranges.
4 Arrange on the lettuce.
5 Put the mustard on to a flat plate and add the seasonings.
6 Gradually blend in the oil and vinegar.
7 Pour over the salad. Arrange round sliced duck.

Hot Puddings

In this chapter you will find a variety of hot puddings, some of them old favourites, others quite new suggestions.

An attractive pudding completes a good meal, and often when people are not particularly hungry and do not eat much of the other courses, they will derive most of their food value from the pudding. It is therefore important that you frequently use recipes which contain milk, fruit etc., so that as well as tasting pleasant, they contain ingredients which will provide real food value.

Pear upside-down cake

cooking time: 1¼–1½ hours

you will need:
for topping:

1 oz. butter	8–10 canned pear
2 oz. brown sugar	halves

for cake mixture:

6 oz. flour (with plain flour 1½ level tea-spoons baking powder)	6 oz. butter or margarine
1 oz. cornflour	6 oz. castor sugar
1 oz. cocoa powder	few drops vanilla essence
	2 eggs
	2 tablespoons milk

1 Melt butter and blend with brown sugar.
2 Spread over base of greased 8-inch cake tin.
3 Arrange pear halves on top, cut sides down.
4 Sift together dry ingredients.
5 Cream margarine, sugar and vanilla essence till light and fluffy.
6 Beat in eggs gradually.
7 Fold in dry ingredients alternately with milk.
8 Spoon mixture over pears.
9 Smooth with a knife.
10 Bake in centre of oven at 350°F. – Gas Mark 3 for 1¼–1½ hours.
11 Serve warm with cream.

Variation:
Peach and cherry upside-down cake – use about 4–5 halved peaches and glacé cherries in place of pears. Add the grated rind of 1 lemon to the butter and brown sugar and the juice of the lemon in place of milk at stage 7.

Apple and lemon croquettes

cooking time: 1¼ hours

you will need:

4 large cooking apples	2 oz. sugar
6 tablespoons fine breadcrumbs	1 egg
	crisp breadcrumbs
grated rind 1 lemon	fat for frying

1 Bake apples in skins, skin and mash while hot, adding crumbs, lemon rind and sugar.
2 Leave until cold, then make into finger shapes.
3 Roll in beaten egg and crisp crumbs.
4 Fry until golden brown.
5 Serve with custard or with lemon marmalade sauce (see below).

Variations:
Apple and rice croquettes – use recipe above, but use 2 oz. cooked rice in place of crumbs.

Apple and ginger croquettes – use either of the previous recipes, i.e. either adding cooked rice or crumbs to the apple mixture. Add 3–4 oz. chopped preserved ginger at stage 1 while the apples are still warm.
Stir about 1 tablespoon preserved ginger syrup into the lemon marmalade sauce or add 1–2 oz. chopped preserved ginger.

Lemon marmalade sauce

cooking time: about 10 minutes

you will need:

juice 1 lemon	1 rounded teaspoon cornflour or arrow-root
3 tablespoons orange or lemon marmalade	
¼ pint water, blended with	

1 Combine all ingredients in saucepan.
2 Boil until clear, stirring well. Taste and sweeten if desired.

Arabian pudding

cooking time: 1 hour

you will need:

1 large cooking apple	1 level teaspoon
4 oz. fat	mixed spice
4 oz. soft brown sugar	¼ level teaspoon salt
2 eggs	1 tablespoon milk
4 oz. flour (with plain	1 glacé cherry
flour 1 teaspoon	
baking powder)	

1 Peel and core the apple.
2 Cream the fat and sugar together in a bowl, until light and fluffy.
3 Beat in eggs thoroughly, one at a time.
4 Fold in the sieved flour, mixed spice, salt and milk.
5 Brush a 6-inch deep cake tin or soufflé dish with melted fat and line bottom with greaseproof paper.
6 Cover this with thinly sliced apple to form a circular pattern and place a glacé cherry in the centre.
7 Place the cake mixture over the fruit evenly.
8 Bake on the middle shelf of a very moderate oven (350°F. – Gas Mark 3) for 1 hour.
9 Turn out on to a hot serving dish.
10 Serve with custard or cream.

Bread and butter pudding

cooking time: 45 minutes

you will need:

3 slices very thin	1 good tablespoon
bread and butter	sugar
1 egg	2 tablespoons dried
½ pint milk	fruit

1 Divide the bread and butter in neat triangles and arrange in a greased pie dish.
2 Beat the egg and pour the warmed milk over it.
3 Add half the sugar and the dried fruit.
4 Pour over the bread and butter and dust the top with sugar.
5 Cook for about 45 minutes in a very moderate oven (350°F. – Gas Mark 3), when the custard should be set.
6 For the last 15 minutes move the dish to top of oven so that the pudding browns and becomes crisp.

Variations:

Orange bread and butter pudding – omit dried fruit, add grated rind of an orange and 1–2 oz. crystallised peel.

Luxury bread and butter pudding – add 2–3 tablespoons cream to egg and milk. Increase amount of dried fruit slightly, add few chopped glacé cherries and a little crystallised peel.

Fruit crisp

cooking time: 30 minutes

you will need:

1 lb. fruit – apples,	1 oz. fat
rhubarb, plums or	2 oz. flour
soft fruit	2 oz. crisp bread-
little water	crumbs or coarse
sugar to taste	oatmeal
1 oz. sugar	

1 Put the fruit with very little water and sugar into a pie dish and heat thoroughly in the oven.
2 Cream the fat and sugar.
3 Add the flour and breadcrumbs or oatmeal. The mixture should now look like sticky crumbs.
4 Sprinkle this on top of the hot fruit and bake in the centre of a moderate oven (375°F. – Gas Mark 4) for a good 30 minutes.

Fruit crumble

cooking time: 35–40 minutes

you will need:

1 lb. fruit*	2 oz. butter or
sugar to sweeten fruit	margarine
3 oz. sugar	4 oz. flour (plain or
little water	or self-raising)

*this recipe is suitable for all fruit.

1 Put the fruit with sugar and very little water into a fairly large pie dish. Soft fruits like raspberries need no water.
2 Heat for about 10–15 minutes.
3 Rub the butter into the flour and add the 3 oz. sugar.
4 Sprinkle the crumbs evenly over the fruit pressing down fairly firmly. This makes certain the crust can be cut into neat slices.
5 Bake in the centre of a moderate oven (375°F. – Gas Mark 4) for about 25 minutes until crisp and golden brown.
6 Serve hot or cold.

Cornflake crumble

you will need:

2 oz. butter
1 oz. golden syrup
2 oz. sugar

4 oz. VERY CRISP cornflakes
1 lb. fruit

Method as for fruit crumble but cream the butter with the golden syrup and sugar. Work in cornflakes. This is particularly good with rhubarb and soft fruits.

Fruit sponge flan

cooking time: 15 minutes

you will need:
for flan:

2 eggs
2 oz. castor sugar
2 oz. flour (with plain flour ½ teaspoon baking powder)

1 dessertspoon water

for filling:

about 12 oz. cooked or canned fruit

¼ pint sweetened juice
1 teaspoon arrowroot

1 Grease and flour an 8-inch, deep flan tin (or 9-inch shallow flan tin).
2 Whisk eggs and sugar until very thick and creamy.
3 FOLD IN the sieved flour and the water.
4 Pour into the flan tin and bake for approximately 10 minutes in a hot oven (425°F.–450°F. – Gas Mark 6–7), until firm and golden brown, just above middle of the oven.
5 Turn out carefully and when cold fill with the well drained fruit.
6 Blend the arrowroot (cornflour could be used instead) with the juice and boil until thick and clear. Spread over fruit.
7 If this looks very colourless, you may like to add 1–2 drops edible kitchen colouring.
8 Decorate with cream if desired.

Lemon apples

cooking time: 1 hour 10 minutes

you will need:

4 good sized cooking apples
1 large lemon
1–2 tablespoons brown sugar

¼ pint water
1 slightly rounded teaspoon cornflour or arrowroot
½ oz. almonds

1 Core apples and slit skin round centre.
2 Put in casserole.

3 Mix grated rind of lemon with sugar and press into centre of each apple.
4 Cover with lid and cook until tender – about 1 hour in moderate oven (375°F. – Gas Mark 4).
5 Remove apples and take off top skin.
6 Scrape any juice and sugar from dish into saucepan.
7 Add lemon juice and water blended with cornflour.
8 Boil together until smooth sauce.
9 Pour over apples and decorate with blanched chopped almonds.

Redcurrant apples

cooking time: 1 hour

you will need:

apples
sugar
butter

redcurrant jelly
thick cream for serving

1 Core and split the skins on large baking apples and fill the centres with a little white sugar and a knob of butter.
2 Bake for approximately 45 minutes at 375°F. – Gas Mark 4.
3 Remove top skins and fill holes with plenty of redcurrant jelly.
4 Put back into the oven for a further 15–20 minutes, during which time the redcurrant jelly will melt and run down the outside of each apple making it pale pink.
5 Pour a little thick cream over each apple before serving.

Rhubarb batter

cooking time: 40 minutes

you will need:

8 oz. plain flour
2 eggs
1 pint milk
water

12 oz. rhubarb
good knob fat
little sugar

1 Make a smooth batter with the flour, egg and milk and water.
2 Wipe rhubarb and cut into small lengths.
3 Heat good knob of fat in Yorkshire pudding tin.
4 Add rhubarb to the batter.

5 Pour into the hot fat and bake for approximately 15 minutes in a very hot oven (450°F.–475°F. – Gas Mark 7–8).

6 Lower the heat and cook for a further 25 minutes until firm and brown.

7 Dredge with plenty of sugar when serving.

Orange custard

cooking time: 1½ hours

you will need:

3 eggs	1 small can mandarin
1 oz. sugar	oranges
grated rind and juice	1 teaspoon cornflour
1 orange	sugar
1 pint milk	

1 Beat the eggs and sugar.

2 Heat the rind with the milk.

3 Pour over the eggs and strain into a shallow dish.

4 Bake for approximately 1½ hours, standing the custard in another dish of cold water, in a very cool oven.

5 Decorate with the orange sections.

6 Serve with thick sauce made by blending the orange syrup from the can of oranges, orange juice with a heaped teaspoon cornflour. Boil until thick and clear, sweeten to taste.

Plum meringue

cooking time: 40 minutes

you will need:

1 lb. plums	extra water
½ pint water	2 oz. rice
4 oz. sugar	2 eggs, separated

1 Put the plums in a saucepan with the water and 2 oz. sugar.

2 Simmer until fruit is soft.

3 Remove plum stones and measure pulp.

4 Add enough water to give 1¼ pints.

5 Add rice and cook steadily until rice is soft, stirring from time to time.

6 Remove from heat and add the beaten egg yolks.

7 Put into oblong baking dish.

8 Whisk egg whites until very stiff and fold in the rest of the sugar.

9 Put into piping bag with ½-inch rose pipe and make lattice work on top of the sweet.

10 Set for approximately 20 minutes in centre of a very moderate oven (350°F. – Gas Mark 3).

Rhubarb charlotte

cooking time: 45 minutes

you will need:

3 oz. margarine	little grated lemon
10 oz. stale bread-	or orange rind
crumbs	(or pinch spice)
2 oz. sugar	12 oz. rhubarb
	sugar to taste

1 Heat the margarine and fry the crumbs until golden brown.

2 Mix with the sugar and fruit rind.

3 Put one-third at the bottom of a dish.

4 Cover with half the chopped rhubarb – no water – but sugar to taste.

5 Cover with next third of crumbs, rest of the rhubarb and sugar and a final layer of crumbs.

6 Bake for about 40 minutes in the centre of a moderate oven (375°F. – Gas Mark 4).

7 Turn out if wished.

8 Serve with cream or custard sauce.

Variations:

With apple – mix rhubarb with thinly sliced apples.

With orange – mix rhubarb with sections of orange.

With cereal – use half crumbs and half puffed wheat or cornflakes.

Apple charlotte – use either thinly sliced apples or thick apple purée instead of rhubarb.

Plum charlotte – use either halves plums or thick plum purée instead of rhubarb.

Caramel sauce

cooking time: 10 minutes

you will need:

2 oz. sugar*	4 tablespoons water

*granulated sugar may be used, but it does not brown so quickly as loaf sugar. It is essential to use a really strong pan.

1 Put the sugar and half the water into the pan.

2 Stir until sugar has quite dissolved.

3 Boil without stirring until sauce is brown.

4 Take the pan off the heat and add remainder of water.

5 Return to the heat and continue boiling and stirring until smooth again.

Semolina and caramel crisp

cooking time: 20–25 minutes

you will need:

1 pint milk or milk and water	2–3 oz. dried fruit – dates, sultanas
3 oz. semolina	1 good tablespoon crisp breadcrumbs
1 tablespoon marmalade	caramel sauce (see page 71)

1 Bring the milk to the boil.
2 Whisk in the semolina and add the marmalade and dried fruit.
3 Cook gently, stirring from time to time, for 15 minutes.
4 Meanwhile, make the caramel sauce.
5 Pour the cooked semolina into a hot greased pie dish and sprinkle over the breadcrumbs.
6 When quite brown, pour the caramel sauce over the pudding.

Variation:

Rice caramel crisp – cook 2 oz. round (Carolina) rice in the milk etc. instead of the semolina. This will take about 20–25 minutes. Continue as the recipe.

Rhubarb crunch

cooking time: 30 minutes

you will need:

1½–2 lb. rhubarb*	4 oz. butter or margarine
2 tablespoons sugar	4 oz. brown sugar
¼ teaspoon cinnamon	1–2 oz. chopped nuts
6 oz. flour (with plain flour use 1½ level teaspoons baking powder)	

*When rhubarb gets older, cook for short time before adding topping.

1 Chop rhubarb into 1-inch slices and put into a well greased pie dish.
2 Sprinkle with the sugar and cinnamon to taste.
3 Mix the flour, butter and brown sugar until like breadcrumbs.
4 Stir in the chopped nuts and smooth down over the rhubarb.
5 Place in the centre of a hot oven (425–450°F. – Gas Mark 6–7) for 30 minutes until brown and crisp.
6 Serve hot or cold. Rhubarb crunch is excellent with ice cream.

Vanilla creams

cooking time: 30 minutes

you will need:

packet vanilla flavoured blancmange or 1½ oz. cornflour and a few drops vanilla essence (or vanilla pod)	2 oz. sugar
	3 eggs, separated
	2 tablespoons cream or evaporated milk
1 pint milk	icing sugar

1 If using vanilla pod, put this into pan with the milk.
2 Heat together.
3 Take out pod and rinse in cold water then put back into jar of sugar.
4 Blend cornflour or blancmange with a little cold milk.
5 Bring rest to the boil with vanilla essence or pod, pour over cornflour.
6 Return to the pan with sugar and bring to the boil, stirring from time to time until thick and smooth.
7 **Remove from the heat** and add egg yolks beaten with cream, and lastly stiffly beaten egg whites.
8 Put into 4 or 5 ovenproof dishes and bake for approximately 20 minutes in a moderate oven (375°F. – Gas Mark 4).
9 Dust with sieved icing sugar and serve at once.

Variations:

Chocolate – use either chocolate blancmange or 1 oz. cornflour and 1 dessertspoon cocoa.
Coffee – use ¼ pint strong coffee and ¾ pint milk.
Rum – omit vanilla flavouring, add 1–2 tablespoons rum, or a little rum essence.

Bananas au rhum

cooking time: 20 minutes

you will need:

1 oz. butter	2 tablespoons water
8 medium bananas	2 oz. brown sugar
juice 1 lemon	3 tablespoons rum

1 With the butter, grease a shallow dish and arrange the halved bananas in this.
2 Blend the lemon juice and water and pour over the fruit.
3 Cover with sugar, and bake for 20 minutes in a moderately hot oven (400°F. – Gas Mark 5); add rum 5 minutes before end of cooking.
4 Serve hot with cream.

Steamed Puddings

A light steamed pudding is quickly and easily made. It is, however, important to remember the following points:

1 Have the water really boiling when the pudding goes into the steamer, except in those cases where the recipe indicates the water should NOT boil.
2 Always fill up with boiling water.
3 Allow plenty of space in the basin for the pudding to rise.

Apple pudding

cooking time: 2–3 hours

you will need:

8 oz. suet crust pastry (see page 76)
1½ lb. apples
sugar
water
dried fruit can be added if wished

1 Line a well greased basin with part of the suet crust.
2 Peel, core and slice the apples.
3 Put into the pastry with a good sprinkling of sugar and enough water to half cover the fruit.
4 Roll out the rest of the dough to form a cover.
5 Damp edges of the pastry lid and press on to the pudding.
6 Cover well.
7 Steam over boiling water for 2½–3 hours, or boil for 2 hours. Steaming gives a lighter pudding.

Variations:

Apple and blackberry pudding – as for apple pudding, but mix apples and blackberries.
Blackcurrant pudding – as for apple pudding, but use all blackcurrants instead of apples. Add sugar, but no water.
Cherry pudding – as for apple pudding, but use really ripe cherries, sugar and about 2 tablespoons water.
Damson and apple pudding – as for apple pudding, but use half damsons and half apples, sweetening well.
Plum pudding – as for apple pudding, but use halved plums, sugar and a little water.
Rhubarb pudding – as for apple pudding, but use chopped rhubarb, sugar and no water. Chopped dates can be added.

Old-fashioned lemon suet pudding

cooking time: 2–3 hours

you will need:

8 oz. suet crust pastry (see page 76)
2 lemons
2 oz. butter
2–3 oz. brown sugar

1 Line a pudding basin with suet crust pastry as described on page 63.
2 Put in the lemons, cutting top and bottom of these so that the juice can flow.
3 Add butter and sugar.
4 Cover with a 'lid' of suet crust pastry and cook as apple pudding.

Halfpay pudding

cooking time: 1½–2 hours

you will need:

3 oz. suet or margarine
4 oz. breadcrumbs
2 oz. flour (with plain flour use 1 level teaspoon baking powder)
2 tablespoons golden syrup
3 oz. sultanas
3 oz. currants
milk or egg and milk to mix

1 Mix together the suet, crumbs and sieved flour. If using margarine, melt this and add in place of the suet.
2 Put in the golden syrup, dried fruit and stir thoroughly.
3 Add the milk or milk and egg to give a sticky consistency.
4 Half-fill a greased basin, cover with greased paper.
5 Steam for 1½–2 hours.

Variation:

With golden syrup – if wished 2–3 tablespoons golden syrup can be put at the bottom of the basin to give a sauce.

Mocha pudding

cooking time: 2½ hours

you will need:

4 egg yolks
2 egg whites
2 oz. sugar
2 oz. chocolate powder
¾ pint milk
¼ pint very strong
  coffee
2 oz. chopped glacé
  cherries

2 oz. chopped nuts
  (optional)
1 oz. finely chopped
  crystallised peel
2 tablespoons sherry
  (optional)
2 oz. sultanas

1 Beat the eggs, sugar and chocolate powder together.
2 Pour over the milk and coffee.
3 Add the rest of the ingredients.
4 Pour into a greased basin and steam gently WITHOUT BOILING for approximately 2½ hours, or bake for about the same time in a slow oven (275°F. – Gas Mark 2) standing the dish in another of warm water.
5 Cover the pudding with well-buttered paper or foil.
6 If serving cold decorate with a little cream and pieces of chocolate.

Variation:
Chocolate orange pudding – omit the coffee in the mocha pudding and use an extra ¼ pint milk instead. Add the very finely grated rind of 2–3 oranges and 3 oz. chopped crystallised orange peel in place of 1 oz. crystallised peel. Decorate with fresh orange, cream and chocolate.

Finger pudding

cooking time: 1 hour

you will need:

3 oz. castor sugar
2 eggs, separated
3 oz. ground almonds
½ teaspoon grated
  lemon rind

good pinch ground
  cloves
¾ teaspoon cinnamon
1½ oz. butter
1 oz. Savoy or finger
  biscuits

1 Blend sugar and egg yolks until creamy.
2 Add almonds, lemon rind, cloves, cinnamon, melted butter and crushed biscuits.
3 Fold in stiffly beaten egg whites.
4 Turn into greased mould and steam gently for 1 hour. Do not allow water to boil rapidly, otherwise pudding will curdle.

Pies and Tarts

The following recipes cover easy-to-make desserts using pastry. To be really successful with your pastry and pastry recipes, keep in mind the following points:

1 Make certain that the pastry is not too thick.
2 If making a covered plate pie, dust the bottom of the pastry with a little flour and sugar, corn-flour or semolina. This absorbs the juice from the fruit and prevents the bottom layer of pastry becoming soggy.
3 To give an attractive appearance to your cooked pie or tart, dust with icing sugar, castor sugar or brush with egg white, or a little water and sugar before baking.
4 If you want to keep the pastry, wrap it in paper or foil and put it in the refrigerator, or you can prepare the pie or tart and leave it in a cool place a day before cooking. Always cover with paper while storing.

Baking pastry 'blind'

Where a recipe states that the pastry should be baked 'blind', it means without any filling. To prevent the bottom of the tart or flan from rising, either put crusts of stale bread or haricot beans on a piece of greased greaseproof paper, removing these about 5 minutes before the flan is quite baked.

Short crust pastry

for all general purposes

cooking time: according to recipe

you will need:

8 oz. flour	approximately 2 table-
good pinch salt	spoons cold water
4 oz. fat*	to mix

*there are many fats and combinations of fat to use.

Choose between:
Modern whipped light fat – use only 3½ oz. only as it is very rich
Pure cooking fat or lard
Margarine – for best results use a table margarine, a superfine or luxury margarine
Butter
Margarine and fat – perhaps the favourite of all – 2 oz. margarine and 2 oz. cooking fat

1 Sieve flour and salt and rub in fat until mixture looks like fine breadcrumbs.
2 Using first a knife and then the fingertips to feel the pastry, gradually add just enough cold water to make the dough into a rolling consistency.
3 Lightly flour the rolling pin and pastry board.
4 If a great deal of flour is necessary to roll out the pastry, then you have made it too wet.
5 Roll pastry to required thickness and shape, lifting and turning it to keep it light.
6 Exact cooking times for pastry are given in the recipes, but as a general rule it should be cooked in a hot oven (425°F.–450°F. – Gas Mark 6–7).

Variation:

Sweet short crust – add about 1 oz. sugar to the flour at stage 1. This pastry can be used in tarts etc. in place of short crust pastry.

Flaky pastry

cooking time: according to recipe

you will need:

8 oz. plain flour	5–6 oz. fat*
pinch salt	water to mix

*use all butter, all margarine, or ⅔ margarine and ⅓ cooking fat.

1 Sieve flour with salt.
2 Divide fat into 3 portions.
3 Rub 1 portion into flour in usual way.
4 Mix to rolling consistency with cold water.
5 Roll out to oblong shape.
6 Now take the second portion of fat, divide it into small pieces and lay them on surface of ⅔ of dough.
7 Leave remaining ⅓ without fat.

8 Take its 2 corners and fold back over second ⅓ so that the dough looks like an envelope with its flap open.
9 Fold over top end of pastry, so closing the 'envelope'.
10 Turn pastry at right angles, seal open ends of pastry and 'rib' it. This means depressing it with the rolling pin at intervals, so giving a corrugated effect and equalising the pressure of air. This makes certain that the pastry will rise evenly.
11 Repeat the process again, using the remaining fat and turning pastry in same way.
12 Roll out pastry once more, but should it begin to feel very soft and sticky, put it into a cold place for 30 minutes to become firm before rolling out.
13 Fold pastry as before, turn it, seal edges and 'rib' it.
14 Altogether the pastry should have 3 foldings and 3 rollings. It is then ready to stand in a cold place for a little while before baking, since the contrast between the cold and the heat of the oven makes the pastry rise better.
15 To bake, use a very hot oven (475°F. – Gas Mark 8) for the first 15 minutes, after this lower the Gas Mark to 5 or 6, or turn the electric oven off to finish cooking for remaining time at a lower temperature.

Flan pastry or biscuit crust (for sweet flans and fruit tarts)

cooking time: according to recipe

you will need:

4 oz. fat*	pinch salt
2 dessertspoons sugar	cold water or yolk 1
8 oz. flour	egg to bind

*margarine or butter is excellent for this pastry.

1 Cream fat and sugar together until light in colour.
2 Sieve flour and salt together and add to creamed fat, mixing with a knife.
3 Gradually add enough cold water, or egg and water, to make a firm rolling consistency.
4 Use fingertips to feel the pastry as in short crust pastry.
5 To line flan, put pastry over case and press down base and sides firmly, then roll over top with rolling pin for a good edge. Decorate edge if wished.
6 Bake in a hot oven (425°F.–450°F. – Gas Mark 6–7) or as stated in individual recipe.

To fill a pastry flan

Make flan as previous recipe. You need pastry made with 6 oz. flour etc. to fill a 7–8 inch flan ring or sandwich tin. If using a flan ring put this on an upturned baking tin, so making it easier to remove when cooked.

Bake the pastry 'blind', see page 74, for about 15 minutes, then remove paper from the inside and you can remove the flan ring too so the outside browns. Lower the heat slightly if wished and bake for a further 5–8 minutes. Allow to cool, then prepare the fruit as for the Fruit sponge flan on page 70. Put the cold fruit into the cold pastry and continue as step 6 in recipe on page 70.

Suet crust pastry
(for savoury or sweet puddings)

cooking time: according to recipe

you will need:

8 oz. flour (with plain flour 2 level teaspoons baking powder)	pinch salt 2–4 oz. finely shredded suet water to mix

1 Sieve flour, salt and baking powder.
2 Add suet.
3 Mix to rolling consistency with cold water.
4 Roll out thinly, as this pastry rises.
5 Line a pudding basin with the dough, leaving some over for the cover.
6 Proceed as individual recipes.

Puff pastry

cooking time: according to recipe

you will need:

8 oz. plain flour	few drops lemon juice
good pinch salt	7–8 oz. butter
cold water to mix	

1 Sieve flour and salt together.
2 Mix to rolling consistency with cold water and lemon juice.
3 Roll to oblong shape.
4 Make butter into neat block and place in the centre of pastry and fold up first the bottom section of pastry and then the top section, so that the butter is quite covered.
5 Turn the dough at right angles, seal edges and 'rib' carefully and roll out.
6 Fold dough into envelope, turn it, seal edges, 'rib' and roll again.
7 Repeat 5 times, so making 7 rollings and 7 foldings in all.
8 Put the pastry to rest in cold place once or twice between rolling it for the last time, and before baking.
9 Bake in very hot oven (to make it rise and keep in the fat). Bake for the first 10–15 minutes at 475°F.–500°F. – Gas Mark 8–9, then lower to Gas Mark 5–6 or turn electric oven right out or re-set to 400°F. to finish cooking at lower temperature.
10 Puff pastry should rise to 4 or 5 times its original thickness.

Apple raisin fingers

cooking time: 40 minutes

you will need:

8 oz. short crust pastry (see page 75)	1 oz. fine cake crumbs or chopped nuts
3 large cooking apples	3 oz. raisins
	1–2 oz. sugar

1 Line square tin or round flan ring with half the pastry.
2 Grate apples rather coarsely and mix with other ingredients.
3 Spread over pastry.
4 Cover with rest of the pastry.
5 Bake for approximately 20 minutes in hot oven (425–450°F. – Gas Mark 6–7) then further 20 minutes in moderate oven.
6 Cut into fingers.

Variations:

Apple date fingers – recipe as above, but add 4 oz. chopped dates.

Apple cheese fingers – recipe as in apple raisin fingers above, but add 4 oz. grated Cheddar cheese to the ingredients.

Cinnamon apple fingers – recipe as in apple raisin fingers, above, but sieve 1 teaspoon powdered cinnamon with flour when making pastry, and add further teaspoon to the cake crumbs.

Lattice apple tart

cooking time: 40 minutes

you will need:

1½ lb. apples, weight after peeling	grated rind 1 lemon
little golden syrup	8 oz. short crust pastry (see page 75)
3 oz. sultanas	

1 Cook the apples with the golden syrup and very little, if any, water, until a thick purée.
2 Add the sultanas when cooked and the grated lemon rind.
3 Line the bottom and sides of a tin or dish, about 1½ inches in depth, with the pastry.
4 Bake this case 'blind' (see page 74) for about 10 minutes in a hot oven (425–450°F. – Gas Mark 6–7).
5 Fill with the apple mixture.
6 Roll out the remaining pastry very thinly and make a lattice design over the top.
7 Continue cooking for approximately 30 minutes in the centre of the oven, but 10 minutes before the end of cooking time, brush the lattice top with a syrup made by diluting a good dessert-spoon of golden syrup with the same amount of water.

Apple star pie

cooking time: 40–45 minutes

you will need:

10 oz. short crust pastry (see page 75)	1 oz. crystallised lemon peel
1 lb. apples (weight after peeling and coring)	sugar to taste
	2 tablespoons apricot jam or lemon marmalade
3 oz. currants or sultanas	icing sugar to decorate

1 Roll out the pastry and use half to line pie plate.
2 Cover with thinly sliced apples, half the currants, lemon peel and a sprinkling of sugar.
3 Roll out the rest of pastry to cover top.
4 Cut out 4 or 5 star shapes with tiny cutter.
5 Put over fruit, etc.
6 Bake for 20–25 minutes in centre of a hot oven (425–540°F. – Gas Mark 6–7), then lower the heat and cook for further 20 minutes.
7 Heat remainder of currants and apricot jam together and put into star shapes.
8 Dust top lightly with icing sugar.

Spiced apple pie

cooking time: 40 minutes

you will need:

1½ lb. apples (weight after peeling and coring)	golden syrup to sweeten
2 oz. sultanas	1 teaspoon cinnamon and ginger
2 oz. currants	6 oz. flaky or short crust pastry (see page 75)
2 oz. butter	
grated rind and juice 1 lemon	little sugar

1 Slice apples fairly thinly.
2 Put into pie dish with the fruit, melted butter, lemon rind and juice, golden syrup and spices.
3 Add very little water.
4 Cover with the pastry, brush with water and sprinkle with sugar.
5 Bake for approximately 20 minutes in the centre of a hot oven (425–450°F. – Gas Mark 6–7).
6 Then lower the heat for a further 20 minutes to make sure apples are cooked.

Pear dumplings

cooking time: 30–40 minutes

you will need:

12 oz. short crust pastry (see page 75)	little apricot jam, mincemeat, marzipan, chopped nuts or brown sugar
4 good sized fairly ripe pears	little sugar

1 Roll out the pastry and cut into 4 squares.
2 Peel and core pears, but try to keep the stalks on.
3 Fill core with one of the fillings.
4 Put on pastry and gather together to completely cover the pear, with the stalks showing.
5 Lift on to greased baking tray and bake for 30–40 minutes until pastry is crisp and golden brown.
6 Sprinkle with sugar.
7 If the pears were 'stalkless' put stalks of angelica in place.

Apricot and pear flan

cooking time: 30 minutes

you will need:

approximately 6 dessert pears	¼ pint water
1 cooked pastry flan case, using short crust pastry (see page 75)	1 teaspoon arrowroot
	2 heaped tablespoons apricot jam
	few blanched almonds

1 Peel and core the pears, keeping them in a weak brine until ready to coat them with the sauce. (For the brine use 1 level dessertspoon of salt to 1 pint water.)
2 Drain and dry the pears well and arrange in the flan case.
3 Blend the arrowroot with water and put into a saucepan together with the apricot jam.
4 Bring slowly to the boil, stirring all the time, and cook gently until thickened and clear.
5 Cool slightly, then pour over the pears and decorate with the almonds.

Blackcurrant whirl

cooking time: 35 minutes

you will need:

6 oz. short crust pastry (see page 75)	1 teaspoon cornflour or arrowroot
1 large can black-currants or about 12 oz. cooked fresh fruit	1 pint really thick sweetened custard

1 Bake pastry 'blind' in flan tin until crisp and brown.
2 Drain the blackcurrants from the juice.
3 Measure out ¼ pint of juice.
4 Blend with the cornflour and boil until thick and smooth.
5 Mark out flan into 6 or 8 equal sized portions and fill them with alternative portions of custard and blackcurrants.
6 Spoon or brush the flan filled with the black-currants with the glaze.

Variations:

With cherries – use canned or cooked cherries and blancmange instead of custard.
With apple and blackberries – omit the custard and fill with alternate sections of apple purée and cooked blackberries.
With mixed fruit – try mixed fruit – or soft fruits – or bilberries instead of blackcurrants.

Lancashire fig pie

cooking time: 1 hour 40 minutes

you will need:

8 oz. figs	2 oz. sultanas or currants
½ pint water from soaking figs	pinch mixed spice
1 level tablespoon cornflour	6 oz. short crust pastry (see page 75)
1 level tablespoon golden syrup or treacle	

1 Soak figs overnight in water to cover.
2 Simmer gently until tender.
3 Lift the figs out of the liquid.
4 Measure ½ pint of this and blend with the corn-flour.
5 Put into the saucepan with the syrup and cook until thickened.
6 Blend with the figs, currants and spice.
7 Line a deep pie plate with the pastry and bake 'blind' (see page 74) for approximately 15 minutes in a hot oven (425–450°F. – Gas Mark 6–7) until golden, but not brown.
8 Put in the fig filling and finish cooking in just a moderate oven (375°F. – Gas Mark 4) for a further 25 minutes.

Lemon meringue pie

cooking time: 1 hour 10 minutes

you will need:

6 oz. short crust pastry (see page 75)	½ pint water
3 level dessertspoons cornflour or custard powder	2 oz. margarine
	3–4 oz. sugar
	2 large egg yolks
	2 lemons

for meringue:

2 large egg whites	2 oz. sugar

1 Line a pie dish with the pastry and bake 'blind' (see page 74) for 25 minutes in a hot oven (450°F. – Gas Mark 7).
2 Blend the cornflour or custard powder with the cold water.
3 Put into a saucepan and cook gently until thickened.
4 Add the margarine and sugar. Remove from heat.
5 Add the egg yolks to the cornflour mixture and the very finely grated zest of the lemon rind and lastly the juice. Return to stove at low heat for a minute or two, to allow eggs to set.
6 Pour into the pastry case.

7 Whip the two egg whites very stiffly and fold in nearly all the sugar.

8 Pile this on top of the lemon filling and dust with the remaining sugar.

9 Bake for 45 minutes in a very slow oven (250°F. – Gas Mark ½), when the meringue should feel firm to touch. Do not bake the meringue more quickly otherwise it will not stay crisp when cold.

Orange flan

cooking time: 25 minutes

you will need:

4 oz. short crust or flan pastry (see page 75)	½ pint thick custard (made with custard powder, or eggs and milk)
3 large oranges	2–3 tablespoons apple jelly

1 Line a flan case with the pastry and bake 'blind' (see page 74) for about 20–25 minutes until crisp and golden brown.

2 Add finely grated orange rind to the custard and spread over the bottom of the flan.

3 Divide the orange into sections, cutting away pith and removing pips.

4 Arrange on top of the custard.

5 Melt the jelly with about 1 tablespoon water and pour over the oranges.

Breton pears

cooking time: 40 minutes

you will need:

4 large ripe pears	little apricot jam
8 oz. short crust pastry (see page 75)	4 cloves, if liked

1 Peel and core the pears.

2 Roll the pastry out thinly and cut into 4 squares.

3 Put a pear in the centre of each square of pastry, filling the hole with apricot jam and a clove.

4 Gather the corners of the pastry up to the top of the pear.

5 Put on to a greased baking sheet and bake for 20 minutes in the centre of a hot oven (450°F. – Gas Mark 7), then lower the heat to moderate for a further 15–20 minutes.

Note: If the pears are very hard, they should be simmered first.

Prune flan

cooking time: 1½–2½ hours

you will need:

6 oz. prunes	½ teaspoon cinnamon
½ oz. margarine	few drops lemon essence or lemon juice
1 tablespoon golden syrup	
½ teaspoon mixed spice	1 tablespoon breadcrumbs
	5–6 oz. short crust pastry (see page 75)

1 Soak the prunes in a very little water overnight or for several hours.

2 Simmer until soft.

3 Then cut with a pair of scissors into small pieces.

4 Put the margarine, syrup, prunes, spices and lemon flavouring into a pan and heat gently for a few minutes until all mixed together.

5 Add the breadcrumbs.

6 Line a 7-inch flan ring or sandwich tin with the pastry.

7 Fill with the prune mixture.

8 Put in the centre of a hot oven (450°F. – Gas Mark 7) and bake for 30 minutes, lowering the heat after 20 minutes.

To make a prune sauce – any prune juice that might be left could be thickened with a little cornflour, i.e. 1 teaspoon to each ¼ pint juice, and served with the flan.

Rhubarb amber flan

cooking time: 45 minutes–1½ hours

you will need:
for flan:
5–6 oz. short crust pastry (see page 75)

for filling:

12 oz. rhubarb	2 oz. sugar
about 2 tablespoons water	2 egg yolks

for meringue:

2 egg whites	2–4 oz. sugar

1 Make and bake the flan case 'blind' until crisp and PALE golden brown.

2 Cook the rhubarb with just the two tablespoons water and sugar until very soft.

3 Mash or sieve and mix with the beaten egg

yolks – do this while still hot so that the egg yolks get slightly cooked.

4 Put into the flan case.
5 Whisk egg whites until very stiff.
6 Fold in the sugar and pile over the filling.
7 For a hot sweet you need only use the 2 oz. sugar for the meringue and bake for approximately 20 minutes in the centre of a moderate oven until the meringue is golden brown.
8 If you wish to serve this sweet cold, then use the larger amount of sugar for the meringue and set for about 1–1½ hours in the centre of a very slow oven (250°–275°F. – Gas Mark ½–1). This makes sure the meringue will be crisp when cold.

Variations:

Apple amber flan – recipe as above, using 1 lb. apples instead of rhubarb.

Plum amber flan – recipe as above, using 1 lb. plums instead of rhubarb.

Almond flan

cooking time: 35 minutes

you will need:

6 oz. short crust pastry (see page 75)	jam

for filling:

1 oz. margarine	1½ oz. semolina
1½ oz. sugar	1 egg
1 teaspoon almond essence	3 tablespoons milk or milk and water
1½ oz. flour	
1 level teaspoon baking powder	

1 Line a flan ring or sandwich tin with the pastry.
2 Spread lightly with jam.
3 Cream together the margarine, sugar and almond essence.
4 Mix together the dry ingredients.
5 Add to the margarine mixture alternately with the egg and milk.
6 Pour the filling onto the pastry case and bake in the centre of a hot oven (450°F. – Gas Mark 7) for approximately 15 minutes.
7 Lower heat for further 20 minutes.

Bakewell tart

cooking time: 35 minutes

you will need:

6 oz. short crust pastry (see page 75)	2 oz. flour
little jam	2 oz. ground almonds or semolina
2 oz. margarine	2 oz. breadcrumbs
2 oz. sugar	1 egg
2 teaspoons almond essence	2 tablespoons milk

1 Line a large pie plate or 8-inch flan ring with the pastry.
2 Spread over the jam.
3 Cream the margarine and sugar together.
4 Add the almond flavouring.
5 Mix all the dry ingredients together and add these alternately to the margarine with the egg and milk.
6 Spread this mixture over the pastry and jam, dust with a very little sugar.
7 Bake in the centre of a hot oven (450°F. – Gas Mark 7) for 15 minutes, then lower the heat for further 20 minutes.

Autumn medley pie

cooking time: 35–45 minutes

you will need:

5–6 oz. short crust pastry or flaky pastry (see page 75)	approximately 1½ lb. mixed fruit (try apples, plums, greengages, damsons)
	sugar to taste
	very little water

1 Make the pastry as directed.
2 Put fruit into a pie dish or pie plate.
3 Add sugar and very little water.
4 Put the pastry on top, decorating the edges.
5 Bake just above centre of hot oven (425–450°F. – Gas Mark 6–7) lowering the heat if necessary.

Pancakes and Fritters

Pancakes and fritters make a delicious sweet, and are popular with nearly everybody. Pancake batter also has the added advantage that it can be made ahead of time. If stored in a screw topped jar in the refrigerator, or in a cool place, it will keep for a day or so, but do NOT whisk hard before cooking. Another time-saving method is to cook the pancakes, then keep them in foil in the refrigerator. When ready to serve them, re-heat in very hot fat on either side. When making pancakes, keep the following points in mind:

1 TRY and keep one pan for pancakes (or pancakes and omelettes).
2 This should NOT be washed, but seasoned well when new, and then wiped out with soft paper or cloth after use. In this way it will not stick.
3 Put a small knob of fat, or little oil into the pan and allow this to get really hot – there should be just enough to cover the bottom of the pan.
4 Pour in enough of the batter to give a layer over the pan – this means tilting it so the batter runs easily.
5 Only JUST COVER the pan – do not have it too thick.
6 Cook rapidly on the bottom side, then turn with a broad palette knife or spatula, or toss.
7 Cook on the second side.
8 Serve as individual recipes.
9 Add more fat for each pancake.

To toss a pancake

1 Hold the pan loosely in your hand, leaving your wrist very flexible.
2 Flick the pan upwards quite briskly – the pancake should rise, turn in the air and drop back again into the pan with the cooked side uppermost.

The secret of a good pancake

1 Using really thin batter, so the pancakes are crisp and not soggy.
2 Quick cooking in a really hot pan.
3 Serving while they are very hot.

Basic pancake batter

cooking time: few minutes

you will need:
4 oz. flour (preferably plain)	½ pint milk
good pinch salt	3 tablespoons water
1 egg	fat for cooking

1 Sieve the flour and salt into a basin.
2 Add the egg and beat well.
3 Add enough liquid to give a sticky consistency and whisk very hard until smooth.
4 Add the rest of the liquid. Always whisk hard before cooking, unless batter has been kept for a day or so.

Rich pancake batter

cooking time: few minutes

you will need:
4 oz. flour (preferably plain)	just under 3 tablespoons water
good pinch salt	1 oz. melted butter or
2 eggs	tablespoon olive oil
¼ pint milk	fat for cooking

Method as for basic pancakes (see above) but add the butter or oil just before cooking.

Buttered pancakes

cooking time: few minutes each pancake

you will need:
basic pancake batter (see above)

for filling:
3 oz. butter	1 teaspoon grated orange rind
3 oz. sieved icing sugar	sugar to garnish
juice 1 orange	

1 Combine ingredients for filling.
2 Make pancakes.
3 As they are cooked, pile them upon a hot plate, spreading some of the butter filling between each and ending with a pancake.
4 Sprinkle with sugar.
5 Serve very hot while the pancakes are soaked in the orange butter.

Lemon pancakes

cooking time: few minutes

you will need:

basic pancake batter   sugar
                                  lemon

1 Make the pancakes in the usual way.
2 Turn each one on to sugared paper.
3 Roll or fold.
4 Serve on a hot dish with slices of lemon and sugar.

Variations:

Fruit pancakes – make the pancakes and put on sugared paper. Fill with hot fruit purée, roll, put on a hot dish and top with icing sugar.

Dutch pancakes – make the pancakes and keep hot. Do not roll them. Just before serving, fold a stiffly beaten egg white into ½ pint whipped cream. Whip lightly. Spread pancakes with jam and the cream mixture. Fold up and top with whipped cream and grated chocolate.

Crêpes Suzette – add an extra egg to the basic pancake mixture. Fill each pancake with an orange mixture made by creaming together 4oz. butter and 3–4 oz. sugar then adding the grated rind of 2 oranges and a little curaçao. Fold pancakes into four over the filling and place in a hot dish. Mix together juice 2 oranges, 2–3 tablespoons curaçao and a little sugar and heat in a pan. Pour over the hot pancakes.

Ice cream pancakes – make the pancakes and keep hot until ready to fill. Fill each pancake with freshly sugared fruit and ice cream or just with ice cream. Serve with cream or with hot chocolate sauce.

Chocolate sauce

Put 4 oz. plain chocolate, ½ oz. butter and 2 tablespoons water into a basin over a pan of hot water and heat until melted.

Apple fritters

cooking time: 10 minutes

you will need:

3 large cooking apples	1 egg
4 oz. flour (with plain flour add 1 teaspoon baking powder)	½ pint milk or water and milk
pinch salt	1 oz. cooking fat or dripping
1 teaspoon sugar	

1 Peel, core and slice the apples into rings about ½ inch thick.
2 Mix the flour, salt, sugar, baking powder and egg together.
3 Add the water and milk.
4 Flour the rings of apple **before** dipping them into the thick batter. This is most important, otherwise the batter is likely to come away from the fruit when being cooked.
5 Heat the fat in the frying pan and when this is really hot, drop in the fritters.
6 Cook quickly for a good minute on one side, turn them over and cook quickly on the other side.
7 Turn the heat down and cook more slowly for nearly 10 minutes to make sure the apples are cooked in the middle.
8 Serve hot, dusted with sugar.

Variations:

Banana fritters – recipe as above, but use bananas in place of apples and cook for 6–7 minutes.

Pineapple fritters – drain rings of canned pineapple well, then flour as stage 4 in apple fritters. Continue as apple fritters, but the cooking time can be shortened slightly, since the pineapple does not require cooking.

Orange fritters – recipe as above, but use oranges in place of apples. Peel thickly to remove the pith and slice into rings.

Plum fritters (and other stoned fruit) – recipe as above. The stone can be removed from the fruit and the cavity filled with soft cream cheese.

Peach fritters – as recipe above, using halved fresh peaches or well drained canned peaches.

Cold Desserts

The following recipes give a good selection of cold sweets. When a sweet is to be served cold, it has the great advantage that it can be prepared beforehand. Indeed, in many cases, the flavour of a cold sweet will be better if it is prepared well ahead of the time it is to be used.

Marshmallow kissel

cooking time: approximately 20 minutes

you will need:
1–1½ lb. fruit	further ¼ pint water
little sugar to taste	4–6 oz. marshmallows
½ pint water	
1 level tablespoon cornflour	

1 Simmer fruit with ½ pint water and sugar until tender.
2 Blend cornflour with the rest of the water.
3 Add to the fruit mixture and cook steadily until thickened and clear.
4 Pour into shallow dish and allow to cool.
5 Top with marshmallows.

Note: Since marshmallows give added sweetness to this dish, do not be too lavish with the sugar in cooking the fruit. Cherries, cherry plums, plums, are ideal for this dish.

Banana and apple whip

no cooking

you will need:
2 bananas	large block ice cream
juice ½ lemon	nuts
3 dessert apples	

1 Skin and mash the bananas with the lemon juice to prevent the fruit discolouring.
2 Halve, core, but do not peel the apples.
3 Grate apples coarsely.
4 Mix fruit with the ice cream.
5 Pile into glasses and top with chopped nuts.

Note: This should be done just before the meal, so the mixture does not become too soft.

Peach royale

cooking time: 5 minutes

you will need:
4 whole peaches or 8 canned halves	3 tablespoons water (with fresh peaches)
2 oz. sugar	1 tablespoon lemon juice or brandy

for filling:
¼ pint cream	little icing sugar
approximately 8 oz. fresh raspberries or strawberries*	few blanched almonds

*frozen fruit can be used, in which case omit icing sugar.

1 If using fresh peaches, heat the sugar and water until a syrup.
2 Poach the halved peaches in this for approximately 5 minutes.
3 Stir in the lemon juice or brandy at the end of cooking time.
4 Allow to become quite cold.
5 Whip the cream very lightly and fold in the fruit and sugar if desired.
6 Pile into the peach halves and decorate with blanched almonds.

Butterscotch puddings

cooking time: 6 minutes

you will need:
2 oz. butter	½ pint milk
3 oz. demerara sugar	chocolate
6 level tablespoons fine semolina	walnuts
	cream to decorate

1 Melt butter in saucepan over gentle heat.
2 Add sugar and fine semolina and stir.
3 Cook gently for 3 minutes.
4 Add milk gradually, stirring all the time.
5 Continue stirring until mixture boils and thickens.
6 Simmer 2–3 minutes.
7 Pour into 6 sundae glasses or individual dishes rinsed in cold water.
8 Chill.
9 Decorate to taste with grated chocolate, chopped walnuts, whipped cream.

Pineapple and lemon soufflé

cooking time: 5 minutes

you will need:

3 eggs
½ teaspoon lemon rind
4 oz. castor sugar
1 medium can pine-
    apple (retain syrup)

¼ oz. gelatine
2 tablespoons lemon
    juice
¼ pint cream

to decorate:

little angelica   cream

1 Separate the eggs and put the yolks, lemon rind and sugar into a basin.
2 Beat until thick and creamy.
3 Measure the pineapple syrup (you need just ¼ pint).
4 Heat this and dissolve the gelatine in it.
5 Add the lemon juice.
6 Cool and add to the egg mixture together with the chopped pineapple, leaving a little pineapple for decoration.
7 Allow to cool and become slightly stiff.
8 Fold in lightly whipped cream and stiffly beaten egg whites.
9 Prepare your soufflé dish by tying a band of buttered paper above the top.
10 Pour the mixture carefully into this and leave to set.
11 Remove the paper with a knife dipped in hot water.
12 Decorate with a little cream, angelica and pine-apple.

Fruit crispies

cooking time: 1¾ hours

you will need:

4½ oz. butter
3 oz. sugar

6 oz. flour (with plain
    flour use ¾ level tea-
    spoon baking
    powder)

for meringue:

2 egg whites
4 oz. sugar (either all
    castor sugar or ½
    castor and ½ icing
    sugar)

fruit in season

1 Cream butter and sugar.
2 Work in flour.
3 Knead well and roll into balls. If mixture very firm add few DROPS milk.
4 Put on to ungreased baking tins – allowing room to spread and flatten.

5 Bake for approximately 12–15 minutes in moderate oven (375°F. – Gas Mark 4) until **pale** golden in colour (do not allow to leave cooking any longer).
6 Remove from oven – reduce heat to 225°–250°F. – Gas Mark 0–¼. Leave oven door open for a time to lose the heat.
7 Whisk egg whites and fold in sugar.
8 Put mixture into piping bag with plain or rose nozzle and pipe rings of meringue round edge of each biscuit. If you haven't a pipe then do this with a teaspoon.
9 Return to the very cool oven for about 1–1½ hours until meringue is very firm.
10 These can be stored in an airtight tin for a day or so until ready to use.
11 Fill with autumn fruits, as suggested below.

Fillings for fruit crispies

1 **Blackberries** added at the last minute to an apple purée so that they are softened slightly but keep their shape.

2 **Diced peaches,** covered with melted redcurrant jelly and cream.

3 **Diced dessert pears,** topped with cream and pieces of ginger.

Meringue apples

cooking time: 2 hours

you will need:

4–5 peeled and cored
    apples

for syrup:

1 pint water
about 2 good table-
    spoons golden syrup
a little lemon rind

for filling:

mixed dried fruit
    OR apricot jam
    OR honey and
    cinnamon

for meringue:

3 egg whites   6 oz. sugar

1 Combine ingredients for syrup.
2 Poach apples in this.
3 Cook gently for about 30 minutes until just tender.
4 Drain and put in flat dish, filling centres of apples with any of the mixture suggested.
5 Make the meringue by beating egg whites and gradually adding sugar, until mixture stands in peaks.
6 Pile over apples.
7 Set in a very slow oven (250–275°F. – Gas Mark ½–1) until meringue is crisp. Serve with syrup.

Tipsy cake
(a pleasant change from trifle)

cooking time: 10–12 minutes

you will need:

1 deep sponge cake	3 oz. crumbled
2–3 kinds jam	macaroon biscuits
2 teaspoons sugar	1 pint custard sauce*
$\frac{1}{4}$–$\frac{1}{2}$ pint sherry or port wine	cherries, nuts, etc., for decoration

*made with custard powder or egg and milk.

1 Cut cake into about 4 slices, cutting across sponge.
2 Put 1 slice into a dish, spread with 1 kind of jam.
3 Add sugar to sherry or port wine and moisten with this.
4 Sprinkle macaroon crumbs on top.
5 Put on second slice of cake, spread with different flavoured jam, the sprinkling of sherry, etc. Continuing like this, using all slices of cake.
6 Pour very hot custard over and leave until cold.
7 To prevent skin forming as custard cools, cover with a deep basin.
8 Decorate with cherries, fruit, nuts, etc.

Rhubarb snow

cooking time: 10–15 minutes

you will need:

rhubarb	sugar
water	egg whites

1 Cook the rhubarb with very little water and sugar until a very smooth purée – sieve if wished.
2 When quite cold fold in stiffly whisked egg whites (allowing 1 egg white to each $\frac{1}{2}$ pint purée).
3 Pile into glasses and serve very cold.

Variations:

Apple snow – recipe for above but use thick apple purée instead of rhubarb purée. Flavour the apples with either grated lemon rind or finely chopped crystallised ginger or powdered cinnamon.

Blackcurrant snow – recipe as above, but use thick sieved blackcurrant purée instead of rhubarb purée.

Sherry plum compote

cooking time: 5 minutes

you will need:

1$\frac{1}{2}$ lb. plums	$\frac{1}{2}$ pint water
3 oz. sugar	2 tablespoons sherry

1 Halve plums.
2 Remove kernels and crack them.
3 Boil sugar and water for several minutes.
4 Add sherry and kernels.
5 Pour over halved plums while hot and allow to become very cold.
6 Serve with whipped cream.

Caramelled pears

cooking time: 15–20 minutes

you will need:

3 oz. sugar	6–8 almonds
$\frac{1}{3}$ pint water	
4 good sized firm, but not too hard, pears	

1 Put 3 tablespoons of the water and sugar into a pan.
2 Stir until the sugar has dissolved, then boil until dark brown.
3 Add the rest of the water and bring to the boil.
4 Peel, core and slice pears.
5 Put them into caramel and cook for about 10 minutes.
6 Serve in glasses topped with blanched shredded almonds.

Spring time pudding

no cooking

you will need:

approximately 6 slices bread	1$\frac{1}{4}$–1$\frac{1}{2}$ lb. stewed fruit

1 Line a basin with thin pieces of bread – make sure there are no gaps in this.
2 Fill the centre with stewed rhubarb and juice, sweetening this well.
3 Put thin slices of bread over the top and a weight.
4 Leave for 24 hours.
5 Turn out and serve with cream or custard.

Note: Make sure you add the juice of the fruit in this sweet since this soaks through the bread or sponge colouring it a delicate pink and making it moist. If you have never made this pudding, you will be surprised just how difficult it is to realise that bread has been used.

Variations:

With raspberries – for a more luxurious sweet, mix the rhubarb with frozen raspberries and line the basin with sponge cake rather than bread.

Summer pudding – follow the previous recipe, but use summer berry fruits, such as raspberries and redcurrants, black and redcurrants, loganberries, etc. Top with plenty of cream when serving.

Winter pudding – recipe as Spring time pudding, but use cooked apples, flavoured with crystallised ginger, seedless raisins, lemon rind and juice.

Chocolate mousse

cooking time: 5 minutes

you will need:

4 oz. bar chocolate 2 egg whites
2 tablespoons milk

1 Melt the chocolate and milk in a saucepan over a low heat.
2 Allow to cool.
3 Add stiffly beaten egg whites.
4 Put into a dish and chill.

Variation:

With orange juice – this is also delicious with orange juice instead of milk.

Using a Pressure Cooker for Puddings

With any pudding containing flour, it is better to steam WITHOUT pressure for the first third of the cooking time, then put on the 5 lb. pressure weight, and allow two thirds of the total cooking time at this pressure. This is to make sure that the raising agent will rise properly.

Coffee pudding

cooking time: 15 minutes

pressure cooking time: 30 minutes

you will need:

2 oz. margarine 2 oz. sugar
4 oz. flour (2 tea- ¼ pint strong coffee
spoons baking (just under)
powder if using 1 egg
plain flour) few drops vanilla
2 oz. breadcrumbs essence

1 Rub margarine into the flour.
2 Add baking powder, crumbs and sugar.
3 Mix with the coffee, egg and vanilla essence.
4 Put into a greased basin, stand basin on rack in cooker in 2 pints **boiling** water and cover well.
5 Fix the lid, but do not put on pressure weight.

6 Steam rapidly for 15 minutes then put on pressure weight.
7 Bring to pressure at 5 lb.
8 Lower the heat and cook for 30 minutes.
9 Reduce pressure at once.
10 Serve with chocolate sauce.

Egg custard

pressure cooking time: 10 minutes at 5 lb. pressure

It is an extraordinary fact that an egg custard, which normally requires such slow careful cooking, can actually be made in a pressure cooker. The following recipe shows how it is done.

you will need:

2 small eggs 1 good dessertspoon
½–¾ pint milk sugar
(depending how few drops vanilla
firm you like the essence, or vanilla
custard) pod

1 Beat the eggs lightly.
2 Heat the milk with the sugar and vanilla essence or vanilla pod (remove this when the milk is heated).

3 Pour over the eggs, then strain into basin or mould.

4 Heat ½ pint water in the cooker, then stand the custard on the rack.

5 Bring up to 5 lb. pressure.

6 Maintain at pressure for 10 minutes, then allow it to drop gradually.

Variations:

Caramel custard – make the caramel sauce (see page 71) and pour into the bottom of the mould, then pour the custard on top when the caramel is cold. Cook at pressure as above.

Coffee custard – flavour the custard with a little strong coffee.

Chocolate custard – blend 1 oz. chocolate powder with the beaten eggs and sugar.

Fig pudding

cooking time: 15 minutes

pressure cooking time: 30 minutes

you will need:

3 oz. chopped figs	2 oz. breadcrumbs
2 oz. margarine or suet	1 oz. sugar
2 oz. flour (with plain flour use ½ teaspoon baking powder)	little grated nutmeg milk to mix

1 Soak the figs overnight, then strain.

2 Rub margarine into the flour or add suet.

3 Mix all ingredients together with enough milk to make a sticky texture.

4 Put into greased basin and cover well.

5 Stand on the rack in the cooker with 2 pints **boiling** water.

6 Cook as for coffee pudding (see page 86).

Savoury Sauces and Stuffings

There is nothing more delicious than a good sauce as an accompaniment to a main dish, or to vegetables. And a stuffing will not only add to the flavour of a dish, it will also help to make it go further. A number of savoury sauces and stuffings are included in the following section. Several of the basic sweet sauces are to be found in other parts of the book, where they appear with individual recipes.

Tomato sauce

cooking time: 10 minutes

you will need:

1 oz. butter or margarine	2 level teaspoons cornflour
1 small onion	½ pint water
1 small apple	salt and pepper
1 small tube or can tomato purée	good pinch sugar

1 Heat the butter and fry the chopped onion for a few minutes, then the grated peeled apple.

2 Add the purée, the cornflour blended with the water and seasoning.

3 Bring to the boil and stir until smooth.

4 Simmer gently for about 10 minutes, taste and reseason adding sugar if wished.

Creamy onion sauce

cooking time: 25–30 minutes

you will need:

3 medium-sized onions	¼ pint milk
water	2 teaspoons cream
1 oz. butter	seasonings
1 oz. flour	

1 Boil the onions in salted water until soft.

2 Lift out of water and chop onions finely – save ¼ pint onion stock.

3 Make sauce with butter, flour, milk and onion stock.

4 Add chopped onions, cream and seasoning.

Apple sauce

cooking time: 10–15 minutes

you will need:

apples	sugar
water	knob of butter

1 Simmer apples with water and sugar to taste.

2 Sieve or beat until smooth.

3 Reheat with knob of butter.

White sauce

cooking time: 5–8 minutes

you will need:

1 oz. butter or margarine	OR ¼ pint milk for panada or binding consistency (to make croquettes etc.)
1 oz. flour	
salt and pepper	
½ pint milk for coating consistency (i.e. to use as sauce)	OR 1 pint milk for thin white sauce (for soups)

1 Heat the butter gently, remove from the heat and stir in the flour.
2 Return to the heat and cook gently for a few minutes so that the 'roux', as the butter and flour mixture is called, does not brown.
3 Again remove from the heat and gradually blend in the cold milk.
4 Bring to the boil and cook, stirring with a wooden spoon until smooth.
5 Season well. If any small lumps have formed, whisk sharply.

Variations:

Cheese sauce – recipe as above, but stir in 3–6 oz. grated cheese when sauce has thickened and add a little mustard.

Parsley sauce – recipe as above but add 1–2 teaspoons chopped parsley.

Hard-boiled egg sauce – make white sauce as above, add chopped hard-boiled eggs.

Mushroom sauce – recipe as above, but before making sauce simmer 2–4 oz. chopped mushrooms in the milk until tender.

Brown sauce
(coating consistency)

cooking time: 5–8 minutes

you will need:

1 oz. cooking fat or dripping	½ pint brown stock
1 oz. flour	salt and pepper

Method as in white sauce (see above). For a better flavour, fry about 2 oz. chopped onion and other vegetables in the dripping or fat first. Strain if wished.

Variation:

Tomato brown sauce – use ¼ pint stock and ¼ pint tomato juice or purée, instead of ½ pint brown stock.

Mushroom stuffing

cooking time: 5–6 minutes

you will need:

2 oz. margarine	2 teaspoons chopped parsley
1 small onion	
4 oz. mushrooms	seasoning
4 oz. soft breadcrumbs	

1 Heat margarine and fry finely chopped onion in this.
2 Add finely chopped mushrooms (stalks as well), crumbs, parsley, seasoning.
3 Work together and spread on slices of meat, or as directed in recipe.

Veal stuffing

no cooking

you will need:

2 oz. shredded suet or melted margarine	4 oz. breadcrumbs
½ teaspoon mixed herbs	1 egg
	seasoning
grated rind and juice ½ lemon	2–3 teaspoons chopped parsley

1 Mix all the ingredients together thoroughly.
2 The cooked meat from the giblets can be added to make a richer stuffing, if wished.

Note: Make 2–3 times this quantity for a large turkey.

Sage and onion stuffing

cooking time: 20 minutes

you will need:

2 large onions (peeled)	1 egg
4 oz. breadcrumbs	good pinch salt and pepper
1 oz. suet	
1 teaspoon dried sage	

1 Put the onions into a saucepan, adding about ½ pint water.
2 Simmer steadily for about 20 minutes, when the onions will be partly cooked.
3 Remove from the water on to chopping board and chop up into small pieces.
4 Transfer to basin.
5 Add all other ingredients.

Variation:

With onion stock – some onion stock may be used instead of the egg.

Index